the
beautiful
balance

MICHELLE WILSON

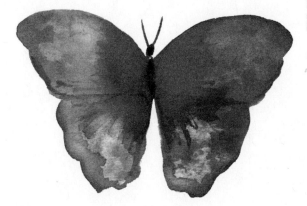

the

beautiful

balance

Claiming Personal Control
and Giving the Rest to God

Covenant Communications, Inc.

Cover image: *Watercolor Butterfly* © Plateresca, courtesy istockphoto.com

Cover design copyright © 2016 by Covenant Communications, Inc.

Published by Covenant Communications, Inc.
American Fork, Utah

Printed in the United States of America
First Printing: August 2016

22 21 20 19 18 17 16   10 9 8 7 6 5 4 3 2 1

ISBN 978-1-52440-090-3

To my parents,
who taught me from an early age to love God.

And to my husband,
because he still gives me his cheesy chips.

Acknowledgments

I MUST FIRST THANK MY husband, Jerey, who supports and loves me even when I write about him in my books. And to my children—Spencer, Paige, and Grace—who bring me such deep joy. Gratitude goes to all the good people at Covenant Communications, especially Kathy Gordon, whose honesty and optimism inspired me, and my editor, Samantha Millburn, who masterfully trimmed and polished until the book became something beautiful. And thank you to Michelle Pipitone for the exquisite cover design. I offer a sincere and deep thank-you to Carol Decker, Bonnie Harris, and Lavinda Hedman for allowing me to share their stories. Thank you to Amy Campbell, Kayla Sainati, Bonnie Harris, McKenna Gardner, Danielle Reid, Jenny Rabe, and many other wonderful friends who have given honest feedback and priceless support. Thank you to my parents, S. Paul and Patricia Steed, for their belief in me. And as always and forever, my deepest love and gratitude goes to God for everything I have and everything I am, and to His Son for access to all that is good.

Table of Contents

PART ONE:

Claiming Personal Control

Chapter 1
The Beautiful Balance

"The best and safest thing is to keep a balance in your life,
acknowledge the great powers around us and in us. If you can
do that, and live that way, you are really a wise man."

—Euripides

The Stormy Day

A FEW YEARS AGO, MY oldest daughter fell sick. The rain and wind angrily pelted the outside of our home in one of the worst storms Washington State had seen in years. Inside, Paige lay on the couch, groaning, pale, and lethargic, with a temperature of 104 degrees. She was rarely ill, so I called the doctor, who urged me to bring her right in. With my husband at work and my young son in school, Paige and I started the trek alone.

The wind rocked my van as I pulled onto the main road. Ominous clouds darkened the sky above; large tree branches and, in some cases, entire trees littered the road below. A downed power line taunted us as we crawled by. I bit my lip in frustration as I edged past a large tree resting on its side, its muddy roots reaching toward the sky. It was a frustrating and painfully slow obstacle course. Paige groaned from the backseat, quickening my already racing heart.

Soon we found ourselves caught in a stalemate with stand-still traffic and debris. My knuckles turned white on the steering wheel. I needed to get her to the doctor! Didn't the people, nature, and the heavens understand? My thoughts turned to my son, who was attending elementary school ten miles away. Frightening scenarios swirled through my mind. What if a tree fell on the school? What if there was an emergency and I couldn't get to him? What if I couldn't protect him because I was trapped here? Frustration turned to panic, and as I looked at the chaos around me, both in the sky and on the ground, my panic turned to helplessness. There was *nothing* I could do. I had absolutely no control.

A dreadful feeling rose inside as the reality of this awful truth sank in. You see, I love feeling in control. I find great comfort and a sense of safety in organizing and maintaining my environment. In fact, the remote control is one of my favorite accessories. With the press of a button, I can turn off what I don't want to see, watch what I want to see, and, because of my awesome DVR, even fast-forward through unwanted commercials. Once, I tried pointing it at my arguing kids. It didn't work. Then I tried pointing it at my thighs to see if I could turn them down—again, nothing.

When I feel like I am in control, I feel safe, at peace. I like knowing I have a say in what goes on around me. But when I feel out of control, I often feel helpless and afraid, like I did in that moment in my van. And I didn't like it one bit.

In the middle of the storm, I wanted control. My daughter was sick, traffic wasn't moving, my son was far away, and I couldn't do anything about any of it. I whispered a desperate prayer that I could do something, anything, to change the situation.

Then came an unexpected answer: *You don't have control.*

That was *so* not the answer I'd wanted. God was supposed to part the cars like the Red Sea or make my daughter's fever disappear or calm the skies or bring back the sun—not tell me my greatest fear of having no control was a reality! Was there anything I had control of?

My thoughts reached beyond my immediate circumstances to all the other areas of my life, such as my children's choices as they grew, my husband's decisions, the totality of my health, my financial situation. I realized I couldn't control any of it. The list of items and events out of my control grew like the thundering storm: the people at church, my neighbors, the stock market, war, famine, or much of anything else for that matter! It felt like everything around me was beyond my control, and I felt terrified.

A rock hit the windshield and brought me back to the moment. I needed to save Paige. In my distress, I had the thought that perhaps God didn't fully understand what was at stake, that if I explained to Him again what I wanted to happen, what I thought *needed* to happen, He would calm the storm and my heart. So, frightened and bit angry, I petitioned Him again with all the faith and feeling I could muster. But the road remained clogged, and the storm raged on. I felt abandoned, hurt, and utterly helpless.

Then another unexpected answer came.

It was not a reprieve from the forces of nature, nor was it the healing of my ailing daughter. In that storm, I was given a piece of heavenly wisdom, one simple eternal principle that settled into my heart and mind: *No, you do not have control over your surroundings, but there is no need to fear. I have given you control over the one thing that matters—yourself. You take care of you, and I will take care of the rest.*

Understanding broke through the black clouds to the reality that everything around me was temporary; however, *I* was an eternal being, and the choices *I* made, the way *I* controlled myself, would determine who I was right then and who I would be when I met the Savior.

In the great intercessory prayer, Jesus prayed for each of us to know a simple yet vital truth: "And this is life eternal, that they might know thee the only true God, and Jesus Christ, whom thou hast sent" (John 17:3). He didn't ask for me to control the stalled sea of cars in front of me or to protect my family from life's storms—He asked only that I come to know Him and our Father. And the way I come to know Them is to become like Them; and the way to become like Them is through the choices *I* make, to embrace the gift of agency I've been given. To claim personal control.

A sense of empowerment began to swell at the latter part of His answer to me. I could also choose to trust God and let go of the rest. I could choose to believe that He really did know what was best in the grand scheme of things, that He was aware of me, my daughter, and the rest of my family, and that He loved us.

That balance of control, I realize now, is one of the fundamentals of a balanced life. As we strive to master ourselves, to grab hold of what we have been given dominion over, with an eye seeking God's will, we can have peace and direction in our lives.

So I did just that: I chose to grab hold and let go of control.

In that moment when all appeared wrong, I felt more right than I had in years. I was excited because in a world of uncertainty, the one certainty I did have control over was the one that mattered most: the power and ability to claim personal control. God was taking care of the rest.

Soon the traffic cleared, and I was able to get Paige the help she needed to return to good health. My son and husband were safe, and all was well. Later, as I pondered that day, I realized everything went back to the way it was—except for me. *I* had changed. I felt stronger, more at peace. I felt empowered and focused. I knew the world would still be a crazy, unpredictable, and scary place I couldn't control, but I had no need to fear, because I knew what I could do and trusted the rest to Him.

High Heels in a Bouncy House

There are times when I lose the focus I gained in my van that day and perhaps even forget the power that lies within me and the heavens above, when I let fear and doubt cast a shadow on my faith in myself and in God. It's especially difficult when I feel like I'm doing the best I can and the world is intent on crashing down around me.

Early one morning, Paige shared a dream that captured what I've felt like so often. She excitedly relayed in great detail random happenings and strange people, most of which my tired brain could not keep up with—until she said, "And then I was wearing high heels in a bouncy house." Though she was referring to herself, an image splashed vividly across the back of my mostly shut eyelids of a stunned, stiletto-wearing woman trying to navigate the unstable vinyl floor of a colorful inflatable structure. Then with a POP!, the bouncy house deflated around her. I chuckled softly. When she strapped on her high heels that morning, I'll bet she wasn't expecting to end up in a collapsing bouncy house.

It might be a funny image, but it embodies the way I've felt more than a few times in my life when I've made plans and had expectations only to have them all fall apart.

For example, I always wanted five children, but medical issues stopped me after two. In my younger years, I dreamed of singing on stage, but God opted out on blessing me with a powerful voice. I wanted to serve an eighteen-month, full-time mission, but an unexpected illness brought me home after only ten months.

In times like those, when I've felt a total lack of control, I've been afraid, frustrated, discouraged, even hopeless. These were the times I felt the most vulnerable. It was hard when what I wanted but didn't get felt good and righteous—things I thought God would want for me too. I wanted to question Him, to wonder why He couldn't just give them to me—especially when I'd worked so hard for them.

Have you ever felt like that? Like you've had no control? When the plans you've wanted just weren't coming together? Maybe now you're in a difficult situation or trying circumstance or perhaps even in the middle of the worst battle of your life. Do you feel like your life isn't turning out like you'd imagined? You might even feel angry, frustrated, or afraid. I would suppose that nearly every one of us has had moments in our lives when we've felt like we've taken the time to prepare ourselves for a night on the town but end up in a bouncy house falling down around us. Sometimes our lives just feel out of control.

Gordon B. Hinckley once said, "I need not remind you that the world we are in is a world of turmoil, of shifting values" (Hinckley, "Stand Strong Against the Wiles of the World"). Turmoil has many origins: forces of nature, illness, economic decline, war, and all manner of awful and difficult-to-understand conditions. President Hinckley puts turmoil on the same plain as shifting values—acts that were once unheard of but are now acceptable. Marriage is being redefined. Laws are twisted and bent. Promiscuity is admired. It seems there is a chasm between the principles of the gospel and the rest of the world—and it is only growing. It's no wonder we sometimes feel like we live in an unstable, deflating house. But life isn't always what it seems.

Looking back I can see His hand in those times that felt like life was going sideways. Yes, I birthed only two children, but God brought my third to me through adoption years later. Yes, my mission was short, but I wouldn't have met my husband if I had served the entire eighteen months. And if God would have blessed me with Adele's voice, I wouldn't have experienced the joy of coming to know Him and myself through study and writing. God knows what He's doing after all.

This is why I love the imagery of Paige's dream. It's humorous and relatable, and it carries with it those eternal and empowering principles I was taught in the middle of the storm: even though we cannot always control our surroundings, we can choose how we adorn ourselves on the outside and, more importantly, on the inside, and we can trust the Lord with the rest.

Finding the Balance

One of my favorite songs is called "Which Part Is Mine." A woman sings about a talent show duet with a young friend, her marriage and mothering, and her relationship with her Heavenly Father. She sings of the struggle to know which part is hers and which part is His. Should she do more or trust more?

I can completely relate to her quest for understanding and balance in life. On the whole, I struggle with balance. In fact, I was just telling someone that I was sure I would die by either a bear, a shark, or stairs. You might look at my list and want to sing the Sesame Street song "One of These Things Is Not Like the Other," but for me, a steep flight of stairs is just as dangerous as a hungry bear or shark on the prowl. I am pretty sure God gave me arthritis in my knees as a precautionary measure against climbing any unnecessarily. Add a pair of heels to a stairwell, and I'm clutching the closest handrail or person to avoid certain death. As much as I dislike elevators, I have come to see them as opportunities to choose life.

Maintaining balance while maneuvering down a questionable stairwell, however, is not as difficult as maintaining balance in other areas of my life. In particular, I struggle with figuring out which part is mine and which part is Heavenly Father's in my life. There seem to be invisible boundaries I continually trip over. I am either too strict or too lenient with my children, too uptight or too lax about finances. At times I rely too much on myself and other times too much on Heavenly Father to solve my problems or make me happy.

My imperfections cause me to struggle with my boundaries. But as I discovered in the storm, claiming personal control—that's my part. Everything else is His. It sounds so simple, but it's true.

This is the beautiful balance of control:

I can control myself.

I can trust God with the rest.

When I do this, I create what I call a perfect companionship with God. We each do our own divine part, helping and loving each other along the way. It is here in this perfect companionship that I find peace and strength because I know that no matter what is happening around me at that moment, everything will be all right.

It's a delicate balance, for sure. There are some who depend too much on themselves and some who leave it all up to others. In 1954, psychologist Julian Rotter developed a concept called the locus of control (Rotter, *Social Learning and Clinical Psychology*). *Locus* is Latin for place or location. Rotter theorized the locus of control was either internal, meaning a person believes they control their life, or external, wherein their lives are controlled by forces beyond themselves, such as circumstances, people, or even fate. He found that people who believe they can control elements of themselves are proactive, while those who think they can't are reactive.

Rotter found those with an external locus of control blame luck, happenstance, and the power of other people. They often lay blame for their failures elsewhere, with bitterness and offense as their frequent companions. *Externals*, as he called them, are often acted upon and don't act themselves; they go with the tide rather than swim their own course. They give up rule over their own spirits and become like a broken-down city without walls (see Proverbs 25:28).

Conversely, he discovered when people believe they have a sense of control in their lives, they tend to be less influenced by the people and places around them. *Internals* experience greater health and success in the workplace and in their personal lives. It is in having that belief and understanding that they have the power and responsibility to mold and create who they are and influence their circumstances for good. These people have more confidence, take responsibility for their actions, and are, on the whole, happier.

I want to make clear here that when I speak of controlling ourselves and having the power to direct our own lives, it is not because we are powerful in and of ourselves. All that we have and all that we are, we owe to God. It is He who has given us the spirit of power (see 2 Timothy 1:7), the ability to act for ourselves (see 2 Nephi 2:16). Though agency is ours alone, it is powered by His grace (see Jacob 4:7), and in this truth, we truly owe all that we have to Him. Ultimately, God knows what is and what can be and who we are and who we can be. If we let Him, He will guide us to where we need to be. When we turn to our Father in Heaven for guidance and support and have faith that He is truly over all, we can ride out any trial, survive any falling bouncy house, and come out better—even perfect—in the end.

When we become partners with Deity, we work and live side by side with Him. Yes, we have big plans for ourselves, but His are bigger. We have big dreams, but His are better. We have an idea of what will bring us happiness, but He knows what will bring us joy. We choose to trade our will for His because we love and trust Him. We walk with Him, rejoice with Him, ache with Him, and become like Him as we do our part and He does His.

But sometimes our control balance is off and we do not even realize it. At times, we might rely too heavily on God. When that happens, we do less ourselves and wait for Him to make things happen. We might pray for work without going to job interviews or pray for blessings without being obedient or pray for success without putting in the effort. It is much like asking a university to issue a degree when you haven't attended any classes. Then when we don't get what we feel should be given us, we get upset with God. People who rely too much on God might also carry the attitude that if God really loved us, He would protect us from the scary situations and bad people of the world, that if He truly cared, He would give us everything we ask for. We are eager to give Him all the power and control as well as all the blame.

On the other hand, when we rely too much on ourselves, we put our own happiness and others' squarely on our shoulders. We often feel the weight of the world bearing down on us. We might try to manage everything around us, from circumstances and environments to people, to ensure our desired outcome. We appoint ourselves saviors and often become angry and blame ourselves when people or things don't turn out the way we've planned. Failure and guilt are our frequent companions.

Buddha once said, "Drop by drop is the water pot filled. Likewise, the wise man, gathering it little by little, fills himself with good" (Buddha, *Dhammapada*). Being imperfect creatures in general, we won't achieve perfect control over ourselves in this life. But each time we choose to be the master of ourselves, drop by drop, our capacity to claim self-control increases. When we focus our mind and heart on God, our ability to claim personal control and give the rest to God grows. Each effort to master ourselves is a drop. Each moment of humble submission is a drop. Drop by drop, with the help of God, we can learn to control ourselves and let Him take care of everything else.

Sometimes medical, emotional, or psychological imperfections might complicate our ability to have as much control over ourselves as we would like. A person who is clinically depressed cannot simply choose not to be depressed. An addict might not, by simply choosing to, decide not to be addicted. Help may be needed from outside sources, such as doctors, counselors, Church leaders, family members, or friends. And that is okay. God has given us these aids because He loves us and wants us to succeed. No matter what our challenges are, with the support of earthly and heavenly resources, we can have the power to fill our buckets of personal control choice by choice and drop by drop. There's always help. There's always hope. And there can be peace.

As we embrace the balance between claiming personal control and giving the rest to God, we find peace in good times *and* bad. We can find perspective and strength in difficult times, feel a reprieve from fears and doubts, and experience the joy that comes from living the life God would have us live. We can find freedom from the burden of being the fixer and savior of everyone around us. We can find focus and purpose. We can find courage and compassion. We can hear the still, small voice of God. We can have a balanced life. As we learn to balance personal control and give the rest to God, we can feel safety and peace in the middle of a storm or a bouncy house or wherever we may be.

Chapter 2
Claiming Personal Control

"The first and best victory is to conquer self."
—Plato

I'm Trying to Slurp . . . Sleep

I AM CONVINCED MY HUSBAND has a sleeping disorder. He can fall asleep within thirty seconds of laying his head on the pillow. It's just not natural. I, however, must go through great effort to fall asleep. This takes the form of a twenty-minute dance routine with my bed and two pillows to find the perfect position all while fighting the urge to get up and take care of just one last thing on my never-finished to-do list. There are some nights when I know divine intervention is the only reason I end up falling asleep.

A while back, I was feeling a heavy load of stress that had begun to affect my already laborious bedtime routine. I would toss and turn for over an hour as I struggled to let go of my ginormous list of incomplete tasks and unmet demands. In my sleep, I would toss and turn with a clenched jaw as dreams filled my mind. Every day I grew more tired and found it harder to fight the feeling that I just couldn't keep up.

One day I decided I needed to take matters into my own hands. I purchased a mouth guard for my teeth-grinding and downloaded a deep-sleep app for my iPad, which promised to lull me to sleep on a soft, fluffy cloud.

That first night, I crawled into my bed, ready for a good night's sleep. I wrote in my journal, prayed with my husband, then waited thirty seconds until he was asleep. I popped in my new mouth guard, plugged in my headphones, turned on the deep-sleep app, and hunkered down under my four layers of blankets. Oh, to fall asleep on a nonclenching, stress-free cloud!

Soft music filled my ears, and I sank deeper into my fluffed pillow. A man's rich Scottish voice wafted into my mind: "This recording is designed to guide you into a deep state of physical and emotional relaxation and down into sleep."

I yawned. Ah, it was working already. Good night's sleep, here I come.

Slurp.

Though my muscles were beginning to relax, my mouth was filling with saliva as it tried to acclimate to the foreign plastic mouth guard. I tried not to drool on my pillow as the Scottish sandman crooned in my ear. "Before going to bed, take some time to make sure everything you need to do is done. This will allow you to fully concentrate on the messages contained within this recording."

A pang of guilt sat me up. "Ha!" I blurted loud enough to nearly wake my comatose husband. *I never get everything finished that I'd like to!* I shouted in my mind. I always began the day with good intentions, but good intentions never seemed to be enough. *And I don't need you to remind me of that. Not cool, Scottish man. Not cool.*

Humph. Slurp.

I closed my eyes, took a deep breath, and lay back down. His voice once again flowed through the earbuds: "For better sleeping patterns, you should go to bed at the same time every night."

Is he for real? He must not have kids.

Slurp.

"Take some time to make yourself comfortable."

Ok. He's trying to make up now.

"It doesn't matter which position you are in in the bed as long as you are comfortable."

My eyes were still closed. *Kiss up—but keep talking. I'm getting tired.*

Slurp.

"Take a nice, gentle, deep breath in through your nose . . . and gently and slowly let it out through your mouth."

I can do that. Breathe. Exhale.

Slurp.

"Take some time to let go of all cares and worries."

I'll try if you stop bringing them up.

I felt slightly sleepier.

Little slurp.

"Nothing matters in this moment. This is your time. No one else's. It's your time. It's time for you."

Yes, yes, it is.

My breathing turned slow and deep.

Drool.

Then sleep.

I awoke three hours later with an earbud in one ear, the cord wrapped around my neck, and the other earbud tangled in my hair. The mouth guard had somehow escaped my clenched jaw and had ended up by my feet. My pillow was moist with drool. But I didn't care. It had worked! I had fallen asleep in a record five minutes!

The next night I tried the routine again.

Earbuds in.

Slurp.

Listen.

Laugh out loud.

Listen.

Slurp.

Fall asleep.

Wake up at three in the morning to the headphone cord trying to strangle me and the rogue mouth guard on the loose.

This was my bedtime routine every night for three weeks. And every night, the same thing happened, except for two changes: one, my mouth grew accustomed to the guard, and I stopped slurping and spitting it out, and two, the more significant thing, I didn't feel that pang of guilt and frustration when I was reminded I should have all my affairs in order—even though I never did.

At first I thought the nightly reminder of my failings would make me feel worse, but the contrary happened. Every night when the Scottish sandman reminded me of my failure, in my mind, I told him it didn't matter. I chose how I would respond and how I viewed my unfinished to-do list. I did what I could—and that was enough. It was okay that my laundry was draped over my exercise bike and there were dirty dishes in the sink. I hadn't ruined my children's or anyone else's lives, and it was okay that I wasn't perfect. It was all right that not everything got done every day. It wasn't failure. It was life.

Now I can actually fall asleep without my Scottish therapist. I don't have the laundry list of my shortcomings whirling through my head or the weight of the upcoming duties of the new day. I am happy. I just fall asleep. No guilt. No Scotsman. No slurping. No headphones trying to choke me. Just deep, relaxing, guilt-free sleep. And it's all because I was reminded of that very important principle: *Though I have the power to influence the world around me and to give my best efforts to do those things I feel are under my obligation, I do not ultimately have control of the world. I can only control myself.* It's not about being perfect. It's about trying drop by drop to do what the Lord would have me do and be who He wants me to be.

In the mortal realm, the only control we really have is self-control, which can be scary—especially when we have so many demands on our time and pictures locked into our minds of how we think life should be. But the concept can be truly empowering. The big question is how can we use self-control for empowerment?

I love to take big things and break them down to a digestible size, then focus on each piece—cake, brownies, and eternal principles, like control. In that light, I'd like to focus on four separate but connected pieces of personal control:

Control over our priorities.

Control over our actions.

Control over our attitude.

Control over our beliefs.

The ability to mold our characters and shape our hearts lies within these four pieces, or realms, of self-control. Herein is where we choose who we are and who we will be when we meet our Savior. And can you imagine what that will be like? One of my most beloved songs asks us to imagine that moment. Will we stand in His presence or fall to our knees? Will we sing hallelujah or not be able to speak at all? I don't know what I will do, but I know what I want Him to do. I want Him to be able to say to me, "Well done, thou good and faithful servant: thou hast been faithful over a few things, I will make thee ruler over many things" (Matthew 25:21). I can only imagine!

Nearly one hundred years before the Savior began His earthly sojourn, the Book of Mormon prophet Alma taught us the importance of a Christlike character and heart. He asked us to, for a moment, take ourselves out of our present situation and "imagine to yourselves that ye hear the voice of the Lord, saying unto you, in that day: Come unto me ye blessed" (Alma 5:16). Alma wanted us to understand that we wouldn't be judged on perfect performance but on the state of our heart. He asked us to imagine that moment when we would face the Savior, then he asked, "Can ye look up to God at that day with a pure heart and clean hands? I say unto you, can you look up, having the image of God engraven upon your countenances?" (Alma 5:19).

We have the power to decide our standing before God and our Savior, not just when we meet Them someday but every day of our lives here. Are we actively becoming like Them? How do we engrave Their image upon our countenance?

The answers to these questions are the same: through the choices we make. As we are good and faithful over a few things, like the four areas of personal control, God promises to someday make us rulers over many things. When we show that we can manage ourselves now, He will trust us to manage more later. We may wish we had control over more than just ourselves, but God doesn't. We may feel that if only we had full control over our environment, other people, and our lives, we'd be happy, but as Elder Neal A. Maxwell explained, "God is infinitely more interested in our having a place in His kingdom than with our spot on a mortal organizational chart. We may brood over our personal span of control, but He is concerned with our capacity for self-control" (Maxwell, "The Tugs and Pulls of the World").

Why is God so concerned with our capacity for self-control? Because He wants us to come home. He wants us to be happy. And as much as He wants to help, He knows the answers to these questions are completely up to us. By our obedience and faith, we qualify ourselves for greater blessings. Not because we have passed some test, but because we will have become more like Him.

Let's take a closer look at each one.

Control over Our Priorities

Time is a finite commodity. There is only so much of it to go around. We spend time and effort on what we decide is important to us, and whether it's physical appearance, our homes, relaxing, family, jobs, etc., they all take a certain amount of time. Our list may be long, and each item may sit at varying degrees of significance. When we are faced with two items on the list, the one that is more important in our eyes (or hearts) will take precedence. Purposefully and prayerfully deciding what is most important will help shape our schedule, our habits, and ourselves.

Eating delicious food—especially chocolate—has always been quite high on my priority list. Sometimes the desire for tasty treats supersedes other important factors—like good judgment. My love of food even drove me to commit all seven deadly sins at an ice cream parlor one night. It was, for all intents and purposes, to be a wonderful evening with extended family. Then someone handed me a spoon, and I took a dare.

At the beginning of the evening, I was in heaven. I had an empty stomach and a wide grin. I was about to eat a beautiful creation called the Daddy Dave's, a half gallon of ice cream topped with hot fudge, nuts, whipped cream, and a cherry. To eat an entire Daddy Dave's is a monumental achievement, one that earns you two badges of honor: a picture on the wall of fame and a bumper sticker.

Many have tried at great cost. But few have succeeded.

My youngest brother, Sam, had two pictures on the wall of fame, and I wanted my picture up there too (*envy*—there's the first sin). He challenged me, and in my arrogance and *pride* (there's number two), I told him I knew I could do it. My priority that night was to claim victory over the tower of ice cream and my little brother.

My entire extended family was there to witness the spectacle. Though I was the first to order, the servers brought out the smaller desserts (for the weak people) before mine. As their beautiful shakes and sundaes were delivered, my mouth watered (*lust*—number three). They all looked so good. Then the waitress brought me my tower of ice cream, and my sweet, youngest daughter reached out her spoon for a taste. I denied it. It was mine (*greed*—number four).

I stared at the tower of dairy goodness in front of me and thought, *Oh, this doesn't look that big. I can totally eat this!* (*Pride* again). By the middle of the mountain, I started feeling unwell. My dad sat next to me with concern in his eyes. "You don't have to do this, Michelle," he leaned in and whispered. "You can stop anytime." As tempting as his words were, I was determined to finish.

Luckily (or not) my husband and my then sixteen-year-old son sat across from me, encouraging me: "You can do it! Just a few more bites!" Inspired by their faith in me, I dug deep and ate it. The whole thing (*gluttony*—a *big*, disgusting number five).

I smiled for my wall-of-fame picture. The smile was easy to see and understand—I'd won the bet and conquered all! But if they had looked closely, they would have seen terror in my eyes. My stomach was starting to revolt. I knew it was going to make me pay, and it did. When I returned home, I lay down and announced I wouldn't be moving for a long, long time (*sloth*—number six). I nursed a soda as I tried to remember why eating that much ice cream had been a good idea in the first place. Just because I *could* do something didn't mean I *should*.

As evening turned into night and the churning in my stomach refused to relent, I grew angry with myself (*wrath*—number seven). Why hadn't I listened to my father, who'd tried to be the voice of reason amidst the dairy inhalation? Why was I so dumb? I shouldn't have eaten it. But I had. I'd eaten an entire Daddy Dave's and committed the seven deadly sins all in one night. It took two days for me to feel well. As much as I love ice cream, I'll never eat a Daddy Dave again.

Now, I don't typically eat entire gallons of ice cream in one sitting, but food is still high on my list of priorities. It has superseded my desire to be skinny and, at times, to practice self-control or moderation. Oh, that elusive *M* word.

When choosing what is important and setting our priorities, moderation is key. Too much of anything is bad. It's imperative that while on our quest to prioritize we seek moderation. There is a line between too much and not enough. Some lines are set firm in concrete while others are pressed into sand. Over the years, my love for food has made the obscure line between accepting myself and improving myself even harder to see. It's a line I have tried to balance, straddle, and hang on to for dear life, only to fall off to one extreme or another.

A few years ago, I was on the "I need to improve myself" side. This phase actually lasted for quite a while. I was consistent with my workouts and watched what I ate. But I wanted more. I joined a weight-loss group that tracked food based on a point-value system and was allowed twenty-two points a day. I counted those points like they were pieces of precious gold. I thought about my points, dreamt about my points, and grew to hate my points. Don't get me wrong, this program has worked miracles for many women, just not me.

For me, it drove me further over the edge of what I thought was self-improvement. I became obsessed. The points were a constant reminder that I would be hungry by the end of the day. They were a constant reminder that I was overweight and I wasn't where I should be. I would wake up in the morning dreading the day. Not only that, but the goal of having a thinner body distorted how I viewed my current figure. I looked at myself in the mirror with complete displeasure. Disgust sounds so negative, but it was close to how I felt. I was quite hard on myself. It also affected my mood. I found I got angry when I didn't eat and angry when I did. No matter what I did, I was angry.

Two weeks into counting points, hating my body, and being angry, I was fed up. I threw away my point tracker and ate a huge bowl of ice cream as a sign of emancipation. Then, like a pendulum at full swing, I threw myself completely into the opposite field. I decided I was going to accept myself, love myself no matter what. I stuffed the scale away and ate intuitively, which is just a lovely way of saying I ate what I wanted. I felt free! I told my husband I didn't need a small waist to feel beautiful. I didn't need strong legs to feel healthy.

As I entered this new phase of self-acceptance, I ate white bread and didn't feel guilty. I ate sweets and chips while watching TV before bed. I ate sugary cereal and my kids' leftover Halloween candy. And I didn't exercise one bit. I was loving it. But only a month and a half into my self-accepting, I realized I felt awful, and if I kept it up, I'd be accepting *twice* as much of me in a year.

I had to take a step back and take an honest look at myself and what had happened. The first mistake was not using moderation in my expectations. As I undertook the self-improvement goal, I had very unrealistic expectations of how I should look and feel. Notice I didn't say *would* look. I had it in my mind that if I was exercising and eating right, if I was being the kind of person I *should* be, then I *should* look like I did when I was twenty. And that didn't happen in the time frame I'd allowed myself. My body didn't change much, but my attitude about it did. No matter what

I did, it wasn't good enough. *I* wasn't good enough because I didn't match up to the extreme expectations I had set.

On the contrary, in hindsight, I realized that when I threw myself into the self-acceptance arena, it wasn't acceptance I really wanted after all; it was permission to abandon self-control. I looked for the green light to eat when I wanted and to have my husband and myself tell me it was all right. I wanted everything to be great without any effort. I wanted what I wanted to be right rather than wanting the right things. Self-control and accountability were not to be found, only self-indulgent behavior. I developed the need for outside validation and acceptance, which I masked with humor and fat jokes, but deep inside, I still felt pretty bad about myself.

As I sat back and realized the wide swing I had taken from one extreme to another, I understood the lesson God had been trying to teach me my whole life: priorities and moderation are key.

There is a line between extremes. It's the Goldilocks perfect place where everything is just right. Even though my initial perspective and priorities were good, I took them to an extreme. And it was too much for me. I had to take a step back to reexamine my game plan. I added a dose of moderation and proper perspective, and voila! I felt better—and I did better. Paul taught the people of Corinth that "every man that striveth for the mastery is temperate in all things" (1 Corinthians 9:25). Self-control and moderation have gone together since the beginning of time.

Our priorities guide our actions. We do and seek after what is important to us. And how we choose to seek these things is important too. When we set goals of an eternal nature as our priority, our lives reflect that choice. What we choose to value affects not only our schedules but the condition of our character and our heart—our very countenance.

But how do we choose what our priorities are, especially when there is so much vying for our attention? The list of requests and responsibilities is long. It is easy to become overwhelmed, as Anne Morrow Lindbergh so eloquently penned: "My life cannot implement in action the demands of all the people to whom my heart responds"

(Lindbergh, *Gifts from the Sea*, 118). How is it possible to tackle everything at church, in our personal lives, at work, at home, and elsewhere? Can we do every single thing that is asked of us?

I submit that we can't. At least, not on our own. It's this way for a good reason—because God wants us to need Him. "The sacrifices that are required of us are of that nature that no man or woman could make them, unless aided by a supernatural power; and the Lord, in proposing these conditions, never intended that his people should ever be required to comply with them unless by supernatural aid, and of that kind that is not professed by any other class of religious people. He has promised this aid" *(Teachings of Presidents of the Church: Lorenzo Snow)*.

We are not meant to be able to do it all. Heavenly Father didn't arrange this so we would feel like failures. He has proposed these conditions as a way to draw us to Him. We need Him to help us. He can and will help us understand what is most important and help us pace ourselves to take care of what He would have us do.

Ask yourself what is important to you. Are your priorities where they need to be? Are you spending time on what is most important? If you're not sure, spend some time with Heavenly Father in prayer. Ask Him. Listen for the quiet promptings to guide you. If you find your priorities need to be adjusted, you can change them. You have that power and that right to decide what is most important in your life. God will tell you if you're right and help you succeed.

Your priorities will be different at different times in your life. Sometimes your priority will be at home with your children, and sometimes it will be making ends meet. You might be caring for an elderly parent or a sick child. The perfectly ironed laundry might have to be wrinkly. Some books might have to go unread. Some people might have to accept help from others God has put in their lives. I can't tell you what your priorities should be. But God can. He can prompt and guide us, and then it's ultimately up to us. We choose what's important. Ultimately, it's in our control.

Control over Our Actions

There are three different kinds of people in the world: those who forgive and forget, those who forgive and never forget, and those who forgive but stay in a bad mood for three days, even after the other person has apologized and moved on.

I've never understood those people who can argue, kiss and make up, and five minutes later act like nothing happened. I used to say I couldn't help it. It was just how I was. Then I had an epiphany a few years ago—I *can* and *should* help it. But it's a lot easier to hold a grudge, don't you think? It's even easier to blame my anger or bad mood on someone else.

Have you ever heard someone say, "Oh, he makes me so mad!"? I know I have. Life can be frustrating. People can be frustrating. It's easy to get discouraged or upset when circumstances don't go your way, when bad things happen, or when people around you make poor choices. But the hard truth of the matter is that regardless of what goes on or how we feel, *we* are responsible for what we do with those feelings. It's up to us to choose how we act in response.

Michaelene P. Grassli once said: "The Lord has given you control of your life by giving you a choice. Let me repeat that. The Lord has given you control of your life. I'm not saying that nothing bad will ever happen to you. You will not always be able to control what others say or do, but you can control how you react to them. Temptation, illness, accidents, and tragedy are part of this life. There will be some tough days in your lives—very tough days. But . . . you can decide what you will say and do" (Grassli, "I Will Follow God's Plan for Me").

That is easier said than done. However, it is not only possible, but it's imperative to our happiness too. I've heard it said that no one can make us feel inferior without our consent. It's our right, responsibility, and privilege to decide how we will respond to outward events. Do we allow others to take us to the brink of sadness? Do we choose to feel offended, maybe even to the point of exclusion? Do we avoid or punish people because we are mad? Do we give others power over what we feel and what we do about how we feel?

Years ago a friend of mine had a young daughter with a small group of friends. One of the mothers decided the group should be smaller and told my friend she wasn't to let her daughter play with one of the children anymore. My friend, seeing no need to exclude anyone, especially a six-year-old boy, ignored the demand. The mother grew angry and abrasive and pulled her child away from the group. This worried my friend. She spent years worrying, hoping something would change. She felt responsible for the situation and did all she could to rectify it but to no avail. Her emotions were all over the map, depending on the other woman's mood and responses. It was exhausting.

But she found a freedom when she finally realized she couldn't control this woman or her actions but could control how she responded to this angry mother. She could decide to let go of what was outside of her control and focus on what she could control. She could decide to forgive her rather than wait for the mother to change. She decided to pray for this woman and treat her with love. Regardless of how the mother responded, my friend felt empowered and happy. What a wonderful picture of liberty and joy!

I love Pahoran's example in the Book of Mormon. He was a wise and good governor, and while many supported him, a group of men called the king-men fought to take control of the government. What began as a "warm dispute" (Alma 51:4) turned into a violent civil war. Moroni, Pahoran's chief military leader, fought with Pahoran for the sake of liberty and freedom. While the people fought each other, their outside enemies, the Lamanites, took advantage of their weakened and distracted state and began an offensive attack that led to years of heavy fighting and bloodshed.

Five years into the war with the Lamanites, Moroni sent a letter to Pahoran, asking for assistance. A reply did not come, which resulted in a great loss of Nephite lives. Moroni was filled with anger and wrote another letter condemning Pahoran. Moroni accused Pahoran of neglecting his responsibilities, withholding provisions, doing nothing, and behaving with slothfulness. He went on to call Pahoran to repentance, even threatening him with the sword if he did not offer relief.

Pahoran wrote back with an explanation of his silence. While Moroni had been fighting his battle, Pahoran had been subjected to a rebellion led by the king-men and had subsequently been ejected from the city.

If a friend of mine sent me a scathing letter like Moroni's—especially if I was in such a tough position myself—it would be hard not to be offended or hurt. And that reaction could be easily justified, right? But Pahoran chose to respond with not only love but also admiration for Moroni. He wrote, "And now, in your epistle you have censured me, but it mattereth not; I am not angry, but do rejoice in the greatness of your heart" (Alma 61:9).

Pahoran was a man who owned himself and his reactions. He understood that power comes from living in the space between stimulus and reaction—it's that space between what happens to us and how we respond to it. I imagine this space as an empty room illuminated by the light that streams in through the giant windows. It's like a control room, the place where I make my decisions. Through the windows of my control room, I can see the stimulus— the arguing children, the angry coworker, the milk spilled on the floor, the shoe the dog chewed up. Rather than *reacting* to what is going on, I can take a deep breath and retreat to my control room, where I see the stimuli from a safe place and choose the most appropriate course of action.

Sometimes this space feels very small to me. Like when I get my 1:00 a.m. ice cream craving, sneak into the dimly lit kitchen, and trip over my dog, who is lying on the floor in front of the freezer; or when I get cut off in traffic; or when I pull on a pair of my jeans only to find that somehow, mysteriously, they have shrunk. Then there are times when the space seems large, filled with minutes, even hours of deep consideration and breaths. These times often involve major decisions about marriage, family, education, or life. No matter how small or large, our control room belongs to us. In the control room, we learn to control own our actions and motives.

The scriptures are replete with counsel about self-control: "Cease from anger, and forsake wrath" (Psalm 37:8). "A soft answer turneth away wrath" (Proverbs 15:1). We also read, "For behold, ye are free; ye are permitted to act for yourselves; for behold, God hath given unto you a knowledge and he hath made you free" (Helaman 14:30). And the Lord Himself said, "Behold, I gave unto him [man] that he should be an agent unto himself" (D&C 29:35). It is here in our control room that we gain the power to act for ourselves and not be acted upon—by others or even our own carnal side.

Those who make decisions and give responses outside of their control room are reactive. They are not actively engaged in their decisions. These folks allow emotion and desire to rule, often acting in haste, irritation, or anger. We have all seen them on the freeway, in stores (the dark side of Black Friday shopping), in our own families—and perhaps even in ourselves. I'm the first to admit that it can be hard not to be reactive when I am tired, sick, or struggling. I know when I've got a headache, my control room seems to shrink to the size of a shoe box.

Regardless of the reasons or excuses we may have for being reactive, we are still accountable for every choice we make. The Lord said "that every man may act . . . according to the moral agency which I have given unto him, that every man may be accountable" (D&C 101:78). We will be held responsible for the way we choose to act and react to the world around us.

Try an experiment over the next few days. Watch yourself as things come up during the day. Do you react quickly, or do you take the needed time to act purposefully and wisely? Are you short with your family? Do you snap at the dog? Do you make impulsive judgments and remarks about people or circumstances?

If you find you are reacting to life more than acting in life, make a decision to change. Practice going to your control room. While you're there, ask yourself a few questions: What would the Savior have me do? What kind of person do I want to be? Do I know what kind of person I should be? What response will aid in an optimal outcome?

Your control room is also a great place to pray. There have been many times when I've been in a situation where I simply haven't known how to respond. A silent plea for help, guidance, discernment, and patience has made all the difference. Often times all it takes is a moment of stillness and pondering to hear the answer we seek.

I am not a proponent of comparing one's trials to another's. We each have our own burdens to bear and trials to endure. I admit my life is not a compelling survival story. I am not complaining, nor do I desire tragedy to beset me, but there are certain words that seem to take on a greater significance when spoken by one who has overcome a major obstacle. Elizabeth Smart is one of those women who has overcome unimaginable horror. During her nine-month kidnapping ordeal, she was subjected to daily rape and abuse. There were times when she wondered why she was still alive. And yet, in her darkest hour, she made the decision that she wanted to live. Her determination to survive pulled her through.

When asked how she was able to survive that nightmare and her recovery afterward, she named riding her horse, playing her harp, being with her family, and relying on her faith. "All of these things have helped me," she penned in her memoir, "but ultimately, to get better, I simply made a choice" (Smart and Stewart, *My Story*, 302).

What a commanding example of the power of choice! Most of the aspects of Elizabeth's life were horribly out of her control, but her choice to not give up her life, her self-worth, and her faith weren't. "Life is a journey for us all," she wrote. "We all face trials. We all have ups and downs. All of us are human. But we are also the masters of our fate. *We* are the ones who decide how we are going to react to life" (Smart and Stewart, *My Story*, 301).

She made a choice. "Yes, I could have decided to allow myself to be handicapped by what happened to me. But I decided very early that I only had one life and that I wasn't going to waste it" (Smart and Stewart, *My Story*, 301).

The idea that growth and freedom stem from choices is liberating and empowering. Our progress and ultimate happiness don't lie in others' hands. They are ours to claim. It is a life-long endeavor but ours to pursue moment by moment, choice by choice, control room by control room.

Control over Our Attitude

Attitude is closely related to perspective. Perspective is how we choose to see ourselves and the world around us. Attitude is the emotion we allow to accompany the perspective we've chosen.

Imagine yourself in a classroom, in the back row, and take a look around. Can you see what the room would look like from that vantage point?

Now place yourself in front of the classroom. Can you see the same room differently? That is perspective. It is the vantage point from which we view the world and ourselves.

Attitude—for the purpose of this book—is the way we choose to *feel* as we view life from that certain point or perspective. Two people can be standing in a line at the grocery store, and while one is happy to have the means to buy food, the other could be angry that the teller isn't moving faster. One person has a good attitude, and the other doesn't.

Of his time as a concentration-camp survivor, Viktor E. Frankl said, "We who lived in concentration camps can remember the men who walked through the huts comforting others, giving away their last piece of bread. They may have been few in number, but they offer sufficient proof that everything can be taken from a man but one thing: the last of the human freedoms—to choose one's attitude in any given set of circumstances" (Frankl, *Man's Search for Meaning*, 104). He likened choosing our own attitude to "choosing one's own way." That's the power of attitude!

Life is full of challenges for all of us. No one is immune or spared. The Savior taught that God "maketh his sun to rise on the evil and on the good, and sendeth rain on the just and on the unjust" (Matthew 5:45). The rich and poor, good and evil, fat and skinny, old and young—everyone will, at some point in their lives, feel the rain pour down upon them. When tough times come, it might be easy to wish our troubles would simply disappear. Wouldn't life be better without all the hassle? In some ways, maybe. But we wouldn't be better. President Spencer W. Kimball said:

> Is there not wisdom in his giving us trials that we might rise above them, responsibilities that we might achieve, work to harden our muscles, sorrows to try our souls? Are we not exposed to temptations to test our strength, sickness that we might learn patience, death that we might be immortalized and glorified? . . .
>
> Being human, we would expel from our lives physical pain and mental anguish and assure ourselves of continual ease and comfort, but if we were to close the doors upon sorrow and distress, we might be excluding our greatest friends and benefactors. Suffering can make saints of people as they learn patience, long-suffering, and self-mastery. (Kimball, *Faith Precedes the Miracle*, 97–98)

Everyone in life will experience hard times, heartache, and loss. Thankfully, the flavor of our attitude can change the way our life tastes. Negativity brings out the bitterness, while positivity enhances the sweetness.

I have spoken with many people over the years who, in spite of their efforts to live righteously, have been dealt a difficult hand. Their negative attitude focuses on what they lack, what they feel they deserve, and how their lives don't match up with what they think they should be. It permeates every layer, dampening their mood, their joy, their gratitude, and their resolve.

On the other hand, I've known many who, despite difficult hardships, have chosen to scale the walls of adversity with hope and optimism. Rather than focus on what they lack, they rejoice in the good they have. They claim the right to have joy in their lives (see 2 Nephi 2:25–27), whatever it brings.

The young Elder Joseph B. Wirthlin's wise mother told him, "Joseph, come what may, and love it." In reflecting the meaning of his mother's counsel, he suggests that "she may have meant that every life has peaks and shadows and times when it seems that the birds don't sing and bells don't ring. Yet in spite of discouragement and adversity, those who are happiest seem to have a way of learning from difficult times, becoming stronger, wiser, and happier as a result" (Wirthlin, "Come What May, and Love It").

A wonderful example of the power of attitude is found in the scriptures. A group of believers had fallen into bondage, where they suffered heavy taxation and persecution. "So great were their afflictions that they began to cry mightily to God . . . yea, the Lord did strengthen them that they could bear up their burdens with ease, and they did submit cheerfully and with patience to all the will of the Lord" (Mosiah 24:10, 15).

That is so inspiring. I will be honest. There have been times in my life when the burdens have felt heavy and hard to bear—times when all I could do was cry and eat ice cream straight from the carton. In many of these instances, submitting cheerfully was not on my radar. At least it didn't feel like it at the time. However, submitting cheerfully doesn't necessarily mean to giggle when the punches come. For me, it's more of trusting in the light of God when my circumstances seem so dark; it's trusting that His purpose is divine and will bring me my greatest joy, even if that particular moment is painful.

Note that these people's burden wasn't removed; they were still in bondage. But when they turned to God, their shoulders were strengthened. Then they made the very purposeful decision to have a positive attitude. They didn't just endure; they submitted cheerfully to their difficult circumstances. They *chose* to smile and be happy, even when their burden was heavy.

Speaking of *endure*, the very word has often conjured a picture of painful drudgery. Life must be endured. Endure to the end. We just need to endure our trials. The way it is said at times almost calls for a few additional *U*'s: We must *enduuuuure*. I propose that to endure isn't drudgery but is a decision to be optimistically steadfast in purpose. To endure means we maintain a positive attitude and say, "Come what may, and love it!" (Though our enthusiasm and ice-cream intake levels may vary.)

A young woman named Anne Marie Rose once shared an experience about the power to choose her own attitude. She had trained hard and earned a spot on the girls' varsity volleyball team. Her joy soon turned to disappointment, though, as she spent much of her time watching other more-skilled players play. Anne Marie felt that life just wasn't fair. The disappointment and frustration was too much to bear. Soon after, she left the team.

After she returned to her studies and other obligations, she couldn't shake the feeling of resentment and disappointment. Finally she came to a realization: "I could *decide* to let go of my volleyball experience. I could *decide* to be positive and optimistic about the many good things in my life." As she made this very purposeful decision to change her attitude and let go of the negativity, she felt a change overcome her. "Suddenly the dilemma that had seemed so overwhelming began to fade. I started to feel better about myself. I read scriptures more. I prayed more. I liked other people more. I felt the Spirit reenter my life" (Rose, "Facing Trials with Optimism").

A few years ago, I came across one of the most striking personal examples of the power of attitude. Looking down the barrel of forty resparked a desire to get back in shape, so I began jogging a few times a week. Then, a month before my birthday, I gracefully jammed my pinky toe on my coffee table. Refusing to acknowledge a possible break, I continued on with my life.

Not too many days after the coffee table attacked me, I went for a jog and felt a sharp pain in my foot. I suffered through a few more days of painful denial, then broke down and went in for a doctor's visit, X-rays, and a CT scan. I found out I had a broken toe *and* a broken foot. Double the fracture, double the fun. My podiatrist suggested I wear a medical boot to stabilize my foot. The hard, plastic boot reached up to the middle of my calf and was uncomfortable and restrictive and made me walk lopsided.

I was supposed to wear the boot for a month, but with my bad attitude and rebellious choices, I wore the boot only half the time. At my next visit, my doctor told me I wasn't healing well enough and I had to wear the boot full-time for at least another month.

I didn't like the boot. I blamed nearly all my troubles on it: my back hurt; my hips hurt; my knees hurt; I couldn't work out, so I was gaining weight. I even blamed the bags under my eyes and my gray hairs on the boot. It was a curse, and I was its victim.

One morning while I was standing in the grocery-store checkout line in pain and feeling sorry for myself, a lively older employee asked me about my boot. I grumpily told him I'd run into the coffee table. With a grin, he announced that was a lame story and I needed to get a better one to impress him. His response caught me off-guard. I eyed him up and down to get an idea of what kind of guy would say that to a crippled woman.

That was when I noticed the metal claw where his right hand should have been.

I gestured toward it and asked what his story was. With an even bigger grin, he said, "October 18, 1968. Meat grinder." He told me he'd been eighteen, working two jobs and going to school. He'd gotten tired and had slipped up, getting his metal glove caught in the large, metal grinder. He then told me it was the most amazing experience he has ever had.

"No way," I replied. That couldn't be true.

"It was!" he said. "I was in and out of the hospital and back to work in four days."

He was all smiles as he explained that the timing couldn't have been better; he'd been young and strong, so his body had recovered quickly. "Isn't that amazing?" He beamed.

Yes, it was. But what I thought was more amazing was this man's attitude. He was genuinely happy. He couldn't go home and take the claw off to put his hand back on. It was permanent. But because of his positive attitude, he was happier for it.

I felt about an inch high. I tucked my boot behind my other leg.

He told me what a great conversation piece it had been over the years, how many great experiences he had had, and how many wonderful people he'd met because of it. People like me. Then he smiled again and told me to get a better story about my foot, wished me luck, and turned to help another customer.

As I left the store, my mind stayed on the one-handed man and our conversation. There I had stood, whining about a temporary boot that protected my foot while it healed, and he had happily waved his shiny hook—not even a prosthetic hand but a hook—like it was the best thing ever. And to him, it was, because he saw all the good that had come from it.

His attitude left little room for self-pity and sadness. I knew then that I had to change my attitude. So I did. And when I did, the boot began to look different to me. I began to see it as a way to help me heal, not hold me back.

As my attitude changed, I noticed another change: my level of gratitude. I could see and was grateful for all the good that had come from the boot, from my bones healing to the conversation with the happy man. In one shopping trip, I went from being a miserable victim to a happy and grateful victor. All because of a much-needed attitude adjustment.

As with all things pertaining to our eternal salvation, the power of attitude lies in our hands. We are counseled to "cheer up your hearts, and remember that ye are free to act for yourselves" (2 Nephi 10:23). In a letter Joseph Smith penned from the dimly lit, cramped cell of Liberty Jail, the sorely persecuted and cast-out Saints received the counsel to "cheerfully do all things that lie in our power; and then may we stand still, with the utmost assurance, to see the salvation of God" (D&C 123:17).

Constant dripping will wear away the hardest stone. A constant flow of negativity, even at a drip's pace, has the power to wear away the most solid perspective, testimony, relationship, and happiness. On the other hand, the enabling power of a positive outlook can open the doors to greater joy, understanding, possibilities, and promises.

Will we choose to lean on negativity as a crutch, becoming unhappy victims of an unfair life? Or do we choose a positive attitude, where hope and love, forgiveness, acceptance, understanding, and joy hold us up?

It's not always easy to stay positive, especially when we are hurting, frustrated, or disappointed. There have been times, admittedly, when I have been downright angry with God for allowing me to hurt the way I have. Sometimes life has just seemed so . . . unfair. Why did *I* have to have this trial when it seemed so many others were doing so well?

Then I am reminded of the words I would tell my young son when he whined about the unfairness of life: "If life were fair, you'd wear your sister's underwear."

No, it's not profound, but it's true. If life were fair—in the context that everything is equal—we would not receive the custom, personalized experiences we need to individually reach our greatest potential. Fair, in the Lord's eyes, is not comparably measured. We are given what we need on an individual basis. The great unfairness of life actually comes when we deny ourselves the very blessings He is trying to give us.

When trials come upon us, and they surely will if they haven't already, perhaps we would do better not to focus on *enduring* the trial but rather on our *endearing* relationship with God. He loves us and wants us to feel that love and to love Him in return. He wants to help us, strengthen us, comfort us, and guide us, but He can do that only if we choose to turn to Him. God has given and will continue to give us what we need in this life. However, He will not force us to accept His offerings or make us love Him. Nor will He make us don a positive attitude. He says, "I, the Lord God, make you free, therefore ye are free indeed" (D&C 98:8). We are free to be negative or positive, to stall or to grow, to become bitter or better.

President Thomas S. Monson, a man known for his cheerful disposition, said of the storms of life, "We can't direct the wind, but we can adjust the sails. For maximum happiness, peace, and contentment, may we *choose* a positive attitude" (Monson, "Living the Abundant Life").

We have the power to choose our attitude. And when we go about living, serving, and loving with "a glad heart and a cheerful countenance . . . the fulness of the earth is [ours]" (D&C 59:15–16).

Control over What We Believe

Our beliefs, in a spiritual sense, reside at the very core of who we are. They influence our priorities, our actions/reactions, and our attitude. One of the easiest and perhaps most effective ways to change the above three areas is to change what we believe in.

For example, if we chose to believe cookies were poisonous, we would make it a priority to stay away from them. If someone were to offer us one, we might react by slapping it out of their hands or, at the very least, refusing it. We might develop a negative attitude because, even though we believe they are bad for us, others are eating them without any apparent negative effects. We might even become resentful, or we might become rebellious and choose to eat them anyway.

That belief, whether true or not, permeates all areas we have control of. Now, if one day we were told, and we chose to believe, that cookies were indeed *not* poisonous, what kind of effect would that have on our priorities, our actions/reactions, and our overall attitude toward cookies? It would most definitely bring about a shift in thought and deed and, most likely, our cookie intake.

There is great power, inside and out, that comes from what we choose to believe, but we must first decide what we believe.

I was chatting with a wonderful woman at church one day, and she shared a secret with me. "I don't have a testimony," she whispered.

I was intrigued by her admission. She had been an active member of the Church for as long as I had known her. She had been stalwart in her duties and had rarely missed a Sunday service. Upon further discussion, I learned that in her eyes, a testimony was something you know. She thought that if she didn't *know* certain things, she didn't have a testimony.

I asked why she had continued to come all these years if she didn't have a testimony. She said, "Well, I like the people. They are all so nice. And . . . wouldn't it just be lovely if it were true?"

We talked about the power of choice. She thought for a moment and then said, "I think I know what my problem is now. I have been waiting to know, but I have never *chosen* to believe."

This sweet woman had spent years waiting for the answer to be given to her. She thought knowing would just come at some point. But in most cases, knowledge isn't just given; it is earned. It is worked for and obtained in steps and layers of choice, hope, belief, faith, and obedience. And though she had an element of hope—*wouldn't it be lovely if it were true?*—she never allowed herself to embrace it—*I hope it's true*. Nor did she ever make the vital choice to believe.

When I asked why she hadn't simply decided to believe that it was real, she explained that she had been afraid of lying to herself. What if she was wrong? What if she believed in something that wasn't true or real? So she kept the decision to believe at bay, as well as all the blessings that come from believing, all because she was waiting for someone or something to convince her it was right.

Please understand I firmly believe certain knowledge can come only from God, but in most cases, we must want it enough to pursue it. "The things of God are of deep import; and time, and experience, and careful and ponderous and solemn thoughts can only find them out. Thy mind . . . must stretch as high as the utmost heavens, and search into and contemplate the darkest abyss, and the broad expanse of eternity. . . . If ye do these things, and exercise fervent prayer and faith in the sight of God always, He shall give unto you knowledge by His Holy Spirit" (*Teachings of Presidents of the Church: Joseph Smith*, 267–268).

The key word in the above quote is *if*. The choice is ours.

Lehi, a prophet and father, taught this truth to his son when he said, "And they [mankind] are free to choose liberty and eternal life, through the great Mediator of all men, or to choose captivity and death, according to the captivity and power of the devil" (2 Nephi 2:27).

We are free to choose what we will believe and which path that belief will take us down.

One of my favorite sayings is "What you feed grows." You cannot expect to have a garden full of knowledge unless you plant the seeds of hope, belief, and faith. These are the building blocks of testimony and the only way toward salvation. They are of the same purpose, the same family, but each plays a different role as they build upon each other.

Hope is the recognition and longing for a certain situation, circumstance, outcome, or desire: I *hope* my prayers will be heard. Or, I *hope* my recipe turns out (yes, it always comes back to food for me!). We'll discuss more about hope later in the book.

Belief is more than just hope. Belief is the decision to recognize what you hoped for as true and real without proof. I *believe* my prayers will be heard. The Savior Himself said, "If though canst believe, all things are possible to him that believeth" (Mark 9:23).

This decision to believe not only solidifies our hope, but it also unlocks the power of faith. Faith is acting upon what you believe: I am praying so that I will be heard.

After Jesus cursed the fig tree, He said to the marveling disciples, "Verily I say unto you, *If* ye have faith, and doubt not, ye shall not only *do* this which is done to the fig tree, but also if ye shall say unto this mountain, Be thou removed, and be thou cast into the sea; it shall be done" (Matthew 21:21; emphasis added).

Faith is belief in action. It is a principle of power built on the foundation of belief. Jesus added, "And all things, whatsoever ye shall ask in prayer, *believing*, ye shall receive" (Matthew 21:22; emphasis added).

Hope, belief, and faith are eternally intertwined. Hope casts our eyes toward the closed door: we long for something amazing to appear from behind. Belief turns our gaze into a goal: we want to open that door. Faith is our belief in action: we reach out, turn the knob, and see what is on the other side.

I grew up a member of The Church of Jesus Christ of Latter-day Saints and was taught its precepts and doctrine. I was also taught that I wasn't expected to believe because someone else said it was true but that I should seek my own testimony. As a teenager, that is just what I did. I stretched my mind and thoughts toward heaven and into myself. I pondered what I had been taught and tried to visualize the possibilities. I *hoped* it was all true. I even prayed to know it was true. I also knew I had felt the influence of the Holy Ghost testify to me that it was true. But I had to make the choice to *believe* it was true. I chose to believe, to plant the seed.

In the years since, that small seed has turned into a garden of testimony that is still growing to this day. Some principles are growing in strong belief. Others have flourished into a deep faith, and some have matured into a sweet knowledge of their reality. My garden is truly colorful, diverse, and continually growing and blooming.

Ask yourself, "What do I choose to believe?" Are you allowing yourself to believe in the things you cannot see? Do you let fear dictate your beliefs as you wait for a sudden measure of knowledge to be given to you? Do you choose to believe there is more to life than you can see?

When I was a newlywed, I worked as a receptionist in a medium-sized office. One of my coworkers was a devout atheist. During my employment there, he and I had many talks about God. He wouldn't allow himself to believe that there was a higher power because he did not want to give up the power he felt he had to direct his life. He told me on more than one occasion that he would admit there was a God if he had proof. He didn't want to believe. He wanted to *know*. He had no hope or desire for God to be real. He just wanted the proof.

It appalled him that I could make the choice to believe in something—someone—I couldn't see. I tried to explain that because of my decision to believe, I couldn't *see* God, but I could see His influence in my life, and I could assuredly hear Him. I explained that I couldn't see the air, but I breathed it in, and it sustained my life. But it wasn't enough for him. Finally we decided to agree to disagree, and we moved on to other topics.

When I was close to having my first child, I turned in my resignation at work so I could be home full-time. On my last day, after the good-bye party was over and the cake was eaten (mostly by me), my atheist friend stopped by my desk on his way out the door and paid me one of the greatest compliments I have ever received. He said, "Michelle, I don't know for sure if there is a God or not, but I know you. And if you believe He is real, then He must be."

He'd made a simple choice to believe.

I haven't spoken to or heard from him since. I don't know if he nurtured his seed of belief or let it die, but I do know this—as he spoke those words to me that day, I saw a change in him. I'd like to think it was the settling feeling of peace that belief can bring or the spark of hope that accompanies it. I don't know. But I hope he won't lose that seed of belief to the fear he once had. Just as the Savior spoke to the doubting ruler of the synagogue, I would love to say to my friend, as well as my good friend from church, "Be not afraid, only believe" (Mark 5:36) or these comforting words the Savior spoke to His Apostles, "Let not your heart be troubled: ye believe in God, believe also in me" (John 14:1).

Our beliefs steer our souls and our lives. It is where we point our eyes and our actions, how we set our goals and expectations, and where we find our purpose and worth. What—and who—we choose to believe in and follow is perhaps the most important choice we can make. It doesn't matter what others tell us to believe. We decide . . . and believe it. We decide if we believe in God and His Son. We decide to believe in the miracles of grace and forgiveness. We decide to believe in ourselves. It is our choice and ours alone.

Own Yourself

I was watching a makeover program on TV once where a woman walked on stage after her makeover. She shined with confidence in her new dress and hair and spoke excitedly about how she'd never thought she could look like that. The host said, "Well, you are beautiful, and you should *own* it." Meaning, hold on to it, believe it, take responsibility for it, and be grateful! We have been given the ability to make our own choices, and when used righteously, that ability makes us beautiful and powerful—and we should *own* that!

God knows us better than we know ourselves. He knows us perfectly. He sees us perfectly. He loves us perfectly. And He is more than willing to tell us how He sees us—which is how we *really* are. One of the greatest gifts to ourselves that comes from claiming personal control is the opportunity to believe God when He tells us how amazing we are. God does not lie, so it must be true.

So, what does it mean to own yourself? Here are a few ways, and you can probably think of more:

Own your worth and your potential. Know who you are. Claim the perspective and blessings that come from God! Grab hold of them, and do not let go.

Own your choices and your mistakes. We are not perfect, and that is more than okay. It is expected. Don't make excuses or blame others for your weaknesses, shortcomings, and mistakes. Own your downfalls, repent of them, and move on. Only then will you be free to have forgiveness, growth, and peace.

Own your actions. You choose to be reactive or not. Stop letting others "make you so mad" or letting life get you down. Choose to smile. Choose to be happy. Choose not to blame others for what you do.

Own your trials. Don't blame others. Don't let anger fester and eat at your soul. Choose to become better, not bitter, in the hard times.

Own your triumphs. You are amazing and capable and can do so much more than you give yourself credit for! Allow yourself to feel the joys of a job well done and the thrill of an accomplishment. As you prove yourself to yourself—for there is no proving to God, because He already knows what we can do—enjoy your confidence in your own abilities and use that confidence as a springboard to grow and stretch even more.

Own your love. Don't hold it hostage until others act the way you feel they should. Love as God does—unconditionally. It also means you choose to let yourself be loved by God, others, and yourself.

Own your knowledge. Fill your mind with the good things of heaven and earth. Knowledge is power, and it shines light on fear and ignorance.

Though we have the power to claim personal control and own ourselves, we must acknowledge that the *only* reason we have that ability is because of the power and mercy of God. All credit and gratitude must first and foremost go to Him. Only through the power of the Atonement of Jesus Christ, according to God's great plan of happiness, are we able to choose for ourselves, to learn, to grow, to become like Him. When we claim personal control, it is not a grandiose declaration of self-importance or independence. On the contrary, it is a humble acceptance of the divine power and mandate He has given us and our sincere desire to claim this precious gift. Without God, we would be nothing. But because of Him, we can be everything, if we choose to be.

God gave us the power to choose. I believe He gave us that power, in part, because He wants us to choose Him. Because when we do that, only then can we fully admit our faults so He can forgive them. Only then can we freely see our weaknesses so He can make them strengths. Only then can we see our worth and potential to do what we once thought we never could. Only then will we freely *feel* the joy of loving ourselves! Only then will we be free to become like Him. And it all starts with a simple choice that we can make right now to claim personal control and own ourselves.

It's Not Just about You

Our choices belong to us, but they do not stay with only us. A lack of righteous personal control can cause deep damage and pain and can range from abuse of any kind to deceit, selfishness, violence, or damaged relationships. Now think for a moment about the fruits of righteous personal control: selflessness, humility, patience, service, and more. You don't have to look far to see how one person's choices can affect many.

Our choices extend to our spouses, children, friends, and coworkers. They bleed into our neighborhoods and society. They can create a culture and behavior that can be passed down through generations, for good (faith in God) or for bad (racism). We have a responsibility not only to ourselves but also to those around us to master our passions, choose righteousness, and be the people God intends us to be.

The necessity of claiming personal control is not a new one. Consider the words of Alma as he tried to awaken his people to their sense of duty over two thousand years ago: "Now I would that ye should be humble, and be submissive and gentle; easy to be entreated; full of patience and long-suffering; being temperate in all things; being diligent in keeping the commandments of God at all times; asking for whatsoever things ye stand in need, both spiritual and temporal; always returning thanks unto God for whatsoever things ye do receive. And see that ye have faith, hope, and charity, and then ye will always abound in good works" (Alma 7:23–24).

Here is what Alma counseled, as it fits into the four areas of personal control.

> To choose our priorities (and moderation): *Temperate in all things*

> To choose how we act/react: *Humble, submissive, gentle, easy to be entreated, full of patience and long-suffering*

> To choose our attitude: *Always returning thanks to God, hope, charity*

> To choose what we believe: *Diligent in keeping the commandments of God, asking for whatsoever things ye stand in need of, faith*

Alma taught that as his people claimed personal control, the Lord would bless them, and they would "at last be brought to sit down . . . in the kingdom of heaven to go no more out" (Alma 7:25). He taught that the work of their own salvation was based on claiming their personal control.

Let's switch gears for just a minute. I like gifts just as much as the next girl. In fact, I have been known to tuck a Christmas gift or two for myself under the tree just so I have something else to open on Christmas morning. But there are some things that aren't meant to be given away, like the brownie you just sneezed on. Some things are best kept to ourselves. It is the same with personal control. It is ours and shouldn't be given to someone else.

God doesn't want other people to control us. He Himself does not want to control us—and He won't. He won't take away our agency. That's His gift to us. We are responsible for ourselves. He's got the rest. He can control the elements that make us, the weather that nourishes us, and He can influence us for good, but He will never control *us*. He knows our growth is dependent upon our choices.

Still, people will try to give away their personal control with attitudes such as, "If God wants me to believe, He will show me a sign." We wait for Him to prove to us that He is real when everything around us already shows us He is (see Alma 30:44). We want Him to make us believe, rather than us making the choice ourselves. God does want us to believe, but He wants us to choose to believe. That is the training wheels for our faith. That is how we give our hearts and ourselves to Him—by our choices.

Through the quest of self-mastery, drop by drop, we can live a more purposeful and rich life. The Savior said, "I am come that they might have life, and that they might have it more abundantly" (John 10:10). We are why He came to earth, lived, died, and rose again—so that we could not only become like Him and return to God but that we could also live an abundant life while we are here. Jesus Christ has done and continues to do His part. Claiming personal control is ours. So let's do it.

Chapter 3
Behind the Quest for Control

"I am not afraid of storms, for I am learning how to sail my ship."
—Louisa May Alcott

The Shark Conspiracy

IN THIS CHAPTER, I'D LIKE to take a step back to explore two powerful drives behind our desire to control: fear and hope. Fear, because we want to avoid what scares us; hope, because we want to ensure our desired outcome.

I don't mind spiders or snakes. I don't even mind rats and rodents. I'm okay with a number of wild creatures. But sharks—those are another story. When I dip a toe into open waters, I live the words from the song of the Israelites, "Fear and dread shall fall upon them" (Exodus 15:16).

You see, I know a secret. There is a shark conspiracy. Sharks of all breeds gather in organized and intelligent meetings to discuss the many ways they plan to eat me, and they make bets on whom the lucky shark will be. You don't believe me? That's okay. Neither does my husband. It probably isn't true, but there was a moment in time a few years ago in Hawaii when you couldn't have told me it wasn't.

I accompanied my husband on a work trip to the beautiful island of Maui. There aren't many places I love more than the beach, where I can gaze out at the blue water as it stretches into the horizon. It reminds me of the greatness of God and my own smallness. It settles my heart, rejuvenates my mind, and fills my soul. This was my experience in Hawaii as I relaxed on the beach one day, stretched out on my towel, toes tucked into the warm, golden sand. I felt peaceful, close to God, and happy as pie. Then my husband got the brilliant idea to go snorkeling. I'm not sure why he felt the need to ruin my vacation, but he did.

Being the brave soul I am—or claim to be—I said I'd go with him. With every step into the ocean, my heart beat faster. The saltwater licked my knees, and visions of the Grand Shark Poobah calling the sharks to order filled my mind. I pushed my mask onto my face, hoping it would give me Bionic Woman vision. With a prayer in my heart and a snorkel in my mouth, I launched myself into a new world.

As I followed my husband's fins away from the beach, the sandy ocean floor transformed into a rolling landscape of coral, plants, and fish. The water was clear around me but grew foggy in the distance. I floated on the water, my body rocking softly with the rhythm of the tide as I became lost in this realm of tropical flora and fauna near me. I had always loved the ocean from above, but to see just a sliver of its magnificent scope below left me in awe. A large yellow fish with a mask of black and white, which later I found out was a raccoon butterfly fish, swam near me. He seemed friendly, even inviting. I stretched my hand toward my new friend as he swam toward me, but it was a moment of symbiotic acknowledgment that ended too soon. The fish darted away. He must have sensed something coming. Something dangerous. Out of the corner of my Bionic mask, I saw the shadow of something approaching. It was large and gray and was only getting bigger. The realization struck me that while I'd been bobbing in my aquatic bliss, the sharks had probably ended their meeting and were racing to see who would swallow me first. How could I have been so stupid?

My breath came shallow and fast. I was too far away from the beach to swim for safety and too young to die. A thousand options, from screaming to splashing to playing dead, swirled through my mind. My muscles tensed, and I froze. There was nothing I could do. I stared at it, not daring to take my eyes off it—the shark that was going to floss its teeth with my arms. My heart thumped in my chest like a drum, calling the shark closer. *This can't be happening.* This was the kind of thing I'd only heard about on the news, the kind of thing that happened to other people. And yet, *just like I knew it would happen*, the moment was here. I was going to die or, if nothing else, be dismembered or maimed in some way.

At that moment, floating in the serene blue waters off the shore of Maui, I was in hell. I was completely terrified and angry at my situation. Fear embedded itself in every emotional, intellectual, and physical cranny and stayed there as the shark swam at me. I could see the outline of its body, its fins, and its . . . snorkel? Soon the suspected shark was just feet away, and I could finally see that it was, in fact, an innocent snorkeler. I would live to see another day!

This story is a beautiful, albeit slightly embarrassing, illustration of the power of fear. It can have a strong effect on our bodies and minds. It is also a powerful and invasive force behind our desires to control our lives and the world around us.

Some of what we fear may be valid and feel quite real and dangerous, while other fears may just seem like they are. But all that we fear shares the same core thread: physical, emotional, or spiritual pain for ourselves or others. Fear is invasive and pervasive, cogent and irrational, real and perceived, conducive and destructive. It can keep us from harm or possible opportunities.

I call my fear of sharks an overt fear. This type of fear can cause us to shake in our boots or scream with wild adrenaline. In the same vein, you'll never get me to bungee jump. I've got a friend who works in a haunted forest each year. She spends ten "glorious" evenings every fall scaring the wits out of people. She loves it. "It's fascinating," she says, "to see how differently people react to fear— from laughing to crying to screaming to running away." Once, a very large man punched her—twice! She's invited me a number of times to go through the haunted forest, and I have refused every time for one simple and extremely logical reason: I don't like to be afraid. It's not fun for me. It actually kind of makes me mad.

Years ago, when my husband and I were dating, we went to a huge Halloween haunted forest in Utah. It wasn't fun. I managed to hold it together until the very end when a crazed man jumped out of the trees and chased me while shaking a screaming chain saw above his head. My then-boyfriend did nothing to protect me. He simply laughed and complimented the guy on his flannel shirt, or something like that. I don't quite remember because the moment I saw the smoke coming from the chain saw, I bolted for the exit gate. I didn't want to run, so I did this weird jolty speed-walk-thing while screaming, "Stop it! Stop it right now!" The barbarian chased me for a good thirty seconds before he turned back for more victims. When you are overcome with terror, thirty seconds feels like a thousand years. I was left breathless, angry, and a little embarrassed. I'm fairly confident my reaction was the highlight of both men's nights.

I think about that night and my reaction often. I knew the crazed man's actions weren't real, yet I had to get away. Why was I so afraid? And why did my fear invite anger?

Medically speaking, I know why I was afraid: everything our senses take in passes through the initial guard of our brain—the amygdala. The amygdala reacts to sensory input before the frontal lobe—the thinking brain—has time to analyze what is really going on. This is why friends can startle us or movies can frighten us. Our amygdala doesn't differentiate between friend or foe, fake or real. It senses something out of the ordinary and sends signals to various parts of our body, unleashing endorphins, adrenaline, and whatever else we need in order to escape being cut up into pieces by a chain-saw-wielding maniac. Everyone's amygdala reacts differently. Mine is somewhat hyperactive, while my husband's is obviously not. I know why I was afraid, but the answer to why I was angry is a bit different.

I don't like being frightened because when I'm afraid I feel out of control. When the "shark" was swimming toward me, I felt there was no escape. I froze. I was afraid and angry. When that madman, who was probably a pimply faced high schooler trying to earn money for prom, chased me, I felt like I had absolutely no control over what was going to happen to me, which made me angry, so I ran. I was seeking control of the situation. When he stopped and turned away, I felt better, safer, more in control, even though I was still a little mad.

Though many people may be able to swim in the ocean unscathed or maneuver through a haunted forest without screaming or punching someone, most if not all people feel fear at other times and in other ways. And along with most of that fear is the feeling of a loss of control. Hence, to get rid of fear, we seek for control.

It is the same with covert fear. Covert fear can be the fear of change, heartbreak, or failure. This kind of fear lies in our subconscious and steers many of our daily actions. Because covert fear typically isn't accompanied by a strong, immediate physical reaction, it can be easy to dismiss it. It, however, can also be far more pervasive and invasive. It hums beneath our surface of conscious thought and can drive us to do what we can to avoid or control the undesired outcomes of life. It can motivate us to try to control our children so they won't get hurt, our spouses so they won't hurt us, and our world around us so we can, hopefully, avoid scary results. We may lie, cheat, and steal, or stand motionless in the face of what we covertly fear.

Overt or covert, fear is fear. It is powerful, and it is scary. That is why, in his first inaugural address, Franklin D. Roosevelt said, "The only thing we have to fear is fear itself." And in order to win the battle over fear, we must understand fear.

I will narrow our focus on fear to three questions: 1. Is all fear bad? 2. Is fear a choice? 3. Does God want us to feel fear? Through our exploration of these questions, I hope we will learn a little bit more about fear and ourselves.

Is All Fear Bad?

Is fear bad? In a nutshell, my answer is yes, but there are some who don't agree. They feel that fear is good *if* it compels us toward that which is good for us. This good fear motivates us and empowers us and drives us to do what is good and right, noble and worthy.

Bad fear keeps us from good or moves us toward bad. For example, fear of rejection may keep us alone, and fear of not being forgiven might keep us from praying. Our bad fear can keep us from pursuing good things that are out of our comfort zones. It erodes our faith in God and ourselves, stunts our growth, and dams our potential. It taints the past, robs our present of enjoyment and peace, and holds our future happiness hostage.

I think fear comes down to semantics. For me, bad fear is basically all fear. Fear doesn't come from God (see 2 Timothy 1:7). It was the devil who introduced fear in the beginning. First he tempted Adam and Eve to eat the forbidden fruit, then he told them to be afraid of their new state (see Genesis 3:6–7). God did not give fear to men. He did the opposite. He provided hope through the Savior (see Moses 5:58).

I propose that good fear isn't fear at all but is our conscience, or the Light of Christ. Heavenly Father gave this light to each of us (D&C 84:45–46), and it is the light by which "truth shineth" (D&C 88:7); it is the "light which is in all things, which giveth life to all things, which is the law by which all things are governed" (D&C 88:13).

Along with the ability to inspire, enlighten, and teach, as President Boyd K. Packer explained, "This inner Light can warn and guard and guide." He continued, "If we understand the reality of the Light of Christ in everyone we see . . . and within ourselves, and understand the great challenge that we have—the surroundings in which we live, the danger which sometimes besets us—we will have courage and inspiration beyond that which we have known heretofore" (Packer, "The Light of Christ"). That is pretty powerful stuff! We have within us a guide that helps move us toward what is right and good and away from what is bad.

People are cautious by nature. We look both ways before we cross the road. We don't stroll into a darkened alley where there are a bunch of men wearing masks and holding knives. We all have some sense of what is safe and what isn't, what is right and what is wrong. It is our own common sense; therefore, we cannot attribute our decision to avoid the dangerous completely to fear; it would be negating the power of the Light of Christ and our own God-given intellect!

God has not only given us minds to discern and the Light of Christ to guide, but He has also given us the Holy Ghost to comfort, teach, bear witness of truth, and guide us (see John 14:26). Elder LeGrand Richards once stated, "I would rather have my children and my children's children enjoy the companionship of the Holy Ghost than any other companionship in this world because if they will heed the promptings of that Spirit, he will lead them into all truth . . . and see them safely back into the presence of their Father in heaven" (Richards, "Improvement"). The Holy Ghost can warn us of impending danger or poor choices. He speaks to us in ways we can understand, from a bad feeling to a thought that pops into our minds to others heeding promptings in our behalf.

The influence of the Holy Ghost, the Light of Christ, and our reasoning minds are the tools Heavenly Father has given us to help us discern spiritual, physical, and emotional danger. This is what Paul meant by power and a sound mind (2 Timothy 1:7). Power comes from above, through the Holy Ghost and the Light of Christ, and from our sound mind, which is our ability to think and discern for ourselves. This power and sound mind can help keep us from making decisions that will bring pain and injury . . . that is, if we choose to listen to them.

Now, back to fear.

Fear does not come from God. President Gordon B. Hinckley implored us to "recognize that fear comes not of God, but rather that this gnawing, destructive element comes from the adversary of truth and righteousness. Fear is the antithesis of faith. It is corrosive in its effects, even deadly" (Hinckley, "God Hath Not Given Us the Spirit of Fear"). Fear keeps us from moving to our ultimate goals, makes us feel sick, makes us feel weak, and robs us of opportunities and experiences.

Fear is one of the devil's greatest weapons to keep us from God, growth, and happiness. We are afraid of sharks, so we don't go in the water. We are afraid of heartbreak, so we don't open ourselves to love. We are afraid of looking stupid, so we don't take chances. We are afraid of being unworthy, so we don't pray. We are afraid we will fail, so we don't try. Fear is a tool the adversary uses to rob us of peace, happiness, opportunities, and growth.

Yes, that most definitely qualifies fear as bad.

Is Fear a Choice?

Fear is bad, but it doesn't change the fact that we all feel it. Does that make *us* bad? Of course not! But now that we understand the source of fear, it is imperative we learn to overcome it. Can we simply choose to pass on being afraid, like saying, "No thank you, I'll skip the salad this time. I'm saving room for dessert"? Is fear a choice?

Going back to my near-death shark attack—I mean, brush with a fellow snorkeler—when I realized the reality of the situation, that I wasn't really going to die, I felt like the crisis was averted. But was there ever a crisis to begin with? I had certainly convinced myself there was, and that was enough to put me into the throes of panic.

In the movie *After Earth*, Cypher Raige, a character Will Smith played, shares with his son his own take on fear and the day he gained control over it. With steely eyes and a gravelly voice, he explains that fear isn't real; it lives in our minds and is carried by thoughts of the future. In his world, fear is a story we tell ourselves.

It is a striking notion—fear not being real. The filmmakers capitalized on this intriguing and maybe even controversial idea, making the tagline for the movie: "Danger is real. Fear is a choice."

It brings up a few very interesting elements. While I was floating alone and intact in the water, there was nothing terrible happening to me. But the *idea* that something could or would happen made my feelings take over my entire being. I weaved a story in my mind of what was to come. I put a label on the dark object approaching. I convinced myself my demise was inevitable.

What I felt was very real. I felt it emotionally, intellectually, and physically. If Will Smith would have appeared next to me in that moment and told me my fear wasn't real, I probably would have shoved the snorkel up his nose and fed him to the shark myself. But it turned out my danger wasn't real at all.

As a fan of the power of choice, I submit that we do have some say in whether we feel fear. Yet, I certainly wouldn't like to think I chose to feel the way I did that day. Who would choose to feel terrified? Sometimes fear ignites so hot and fast that we don't have time or the capacity to choose otherwise. Other times we can fan our worry and anxiety with the stories we tell ourselves until the embers of fear scorch our perspective.

I am not prepared or qualified to make a blanket statement that all fear is a choice. There are some who suffer from panic disorders, anxiety disorders, and other conditions that reach far beyond a simple choice to not be afraid. Though God has given us the power of agency, He has also given us wonderful resources, medications, counselors, and other options to help us gain the power and ability to make more choices for ourselves.

We can make the decision now that we will try our hardest to not be afraid of certain events in the future. This removes some of the power of fear and opens our minds to possibilities and experiences we might not otherwise consider. However, it does not guarantee the absence of fear or the very real physical effects of fear when we find ourselves in certain situations.

Perhaps the more important question isn't whether fear is a choice but how we choose to respond to it. That is where the victory lies. Often times the things we are afraid of are actually good and noble: a new job, a new relationship, forgiveness, a career break, having children, raising children. When we are faced with opportunities and situations worth exploring and we find we are afraid, we have a few options: we can let fear keep us from them, or we can move forward in spite of fear.

When I asked my son, Spencer, his thoughts on our response to fear, he said, "You can't be courageous unless you are afraid." His statement brought to mind Lehi's counsel to his son Jacob as they sojourned in the wilderness: "For it must needs be, that there is an opposition in all things" (2 Nephi 2:11). But why opposition? Because opposition allows us to choose. Lehi explained that because of the sacrifice of Jesus Christ, we "have become free forever, knowing good from evil; to act for [ourselves] and not to be acted upon. . . . [We] are free to choose" (2 Nephi 2:26–27). No doubt there were many things that could—and probably did—incite fear for Lehi and his family: a new and strange land, dangerous animals, rebellion from within the family, an uncertain future, hunger, illness, etc. Yet faith and courage were their mantra, goal, and strength. In the face of all that frightened them, they had courage. They chose faith over fear (see 2 Nephi 2:28). Likewise, in our moments of fear, we have the power to choose what we will do. Choosing to do what we feel is good and right despite our fear is not an easy thing. That is why courage requires strength and bravery. In this light, fear is bad, but our response to it can be good.

Moving forward in the face of fear takes nerve and faith. Luckily, we have wonderful tools from God—the Light of Christ, the Holy Ghost, and our sound minds. For me, it helps to see fear as not a part of me but a separate entity, an invader, if you will. When fear rears its ugly head, because it is not a part of me, I have the power to pick it up and move it aside. Though I might not be able to get rid of it entirely, I can work around it, walk past it, and leave it behind. Fear is not *my* weakness but is an intruder I can expel.

One of the choices we can make when we feel fear is not to feed it. There is a phrase I've used many times before: what you feed grows. We certainly can make choices to feed our molehill of concern until it becomes a mountain of fear. We can choose to concentrate and fixate on what we would not like to have happen so much that when anything crosses our path that even slightly resembles it, we are done for. I know people who spend so much time thinking, stewing, and stressing over fearful possibilities that they bring themselves to a state of immobility.

When faced with fear, we can choose not to feed but to starve it.

When my daughter Paige got her permit to drive, it was a time of learning for her and considerable praying for me. I, on more than one occasion, pressed the invisible brake pedal on the passenger side of our car. On one of her first drives, we started in a parking lot, where she did great—smooth turns, soft braking. Then I asked her to pull onto the street. She froze behind the wheel. "I can't," she said. "I'm afraid."

"Afraid of what?" I asked.

"Everything."

I convinced her to just start down the road. It was a small road with little traffic. As she tapped ever so gently on the gas, she muttered, "I hate this. I hate this. I'm gonna die. I hate this." Talk about the stories we tell ourselves! She was afraid, no doubt about it. And she was feeding her fear giant handfuls of grim absolutes. After a few words of encouragement and direction from me—lovely, maternal, and wise words like, "Quite whining and just drive"—she was still afraid.

I asked her, "Paige, how are you feeling right now?"

"Terrified."

"Is anything bad happening to you at this moment?"

"Well . . . no."

Pointing out at the empty road, I asked, "Can you see any imminent danger?"

"No."

She began to ease her grip on the steering wheel.

I continued. "This can be a wonderful moment if you let it be. Look around. It is a beautiful, sunny day outside. You are doing the same exact thing you did happily in the parking lot just a few minutes ago. You are excited about getting your license. Stop saying you hate this and you're afraid. Let go of the fear of what you think *might* happen, and enjoy the moment you are in."

She took a deep breath and even cracked a smile as she continued to drive. She was enjoying the moment. A car passed, and we had multiple brushes with the side of the road, all of which heightened her anxiety level, but the fact that she had made a *purposeful* choice to not feed the fear was a triumph for her. Even though the fear did not completely abate, she experienced for herself the power she had to either feed or reduce her own fear.

We have the capacity to create our own stories. We have the ability to make our own choices. Fear is real, and we can be guaranteed the adversary will try to wield it in our lives. We may feel overwhelmed and afraid, and that fear might drive us to grasp for control, for something that will help us feel unafraid, but take to heart the truth the Old Testament prophet Elisha once taught. He awoke one morning to find himself and his servant surrounded by an entire Syrian army determined to kill them. His servant, who I can bet was terrified, said, "Alas, my master! How shall we do?" (2 Kings 6:15). I wonder if the biblical version is simply paraphrasing his reaction. I can see it being more along the lines of, "Holy cow! We're surrounded. There's just two of us. There's no way out! We're gonna die! What on earth are we going to do?"

Elisha's response was simple: "Fear not: for they that be with us are more than they that be with them" (2 Kings 6:16). It is true. We have God and Jesus Christ on our side. And they are more powerful than the devil, hands down. Someday I'd like to think we will have the faith and perspective to be completely fearless, but until then, we can choose how we respond to fear when it invades our lives. When it comes, we can ask it to leave. We can feed it or starve it. We can tell ourselves a different story—a story without fear. And that is an empowering feeling!

Does God Want Us to Live in Fear?

In 2001 I had an oophorectomy, which is the removal of not just the "oven" but the entire kitchen—or, in other words, a total hysterectomy. Just days before on my final pre-op appointment, my doctor told me the recovery should be quick; his own wife had been back to work just ten days after her surgery. Still, I was scared. The night before, I prayed for strength and perspective. Through a priesthood blessing, I was given a reassurance that everything would be okay, that He had a plan for me and I was not to be afraid. Of course I felt better.

The next morning, I changed out of my clothes into the high-fashion hospital robe. There was a woman in the stall next to me preparing for a sinus surgery. When I told her what I was going in for, she said, "Oh no! I had a hysterectomy years ago and got the worst infection afterward. It was the worst pain of my entire life. I almost died!" Yeah. Sometimes sharing isn't caring. When they wheeled me into the operating room, I was nervous. But unafraid. God would protect me. Everything would be okay. He told me so.

My recovery, however, was not as swift as my good doctor's wife's. There was a lot of pain and fatigue. Finally, on day twelve, when I should have been back to normal activity, I was in a bad way. My husband took the kids to the park so I could get some rest. I was supposed to have been napping, but instead I was crying. I knew something was wrong with me, but I couldn't believe it. That was when the bleeding started and didn't stop. My head was already on fire, and my clothes were damp with sweat. I cleaned myself and climbed back into bed. I knew exactly what was going on. I had an infection, and it was bad.

I was so sick, so weak, so scared. I knew I needed to get back to the hospital for another surgery. If I didn't, I could die. But I had barely enough energy just to make it to the bathroom and back to bed. There was no way I could make it out of the house, and there was absolutely no way I could endure another surgery. I was too weak physically, emotionally, and spiritually. So I lay there and prayed. I told God I couldn't do it. I prayed for my kids and my husband. I wept as I thought of them going on without me, but in my exhaustion, I couldn't see another way. I was scared and angry. It wasn't supposed to be this way. I was supposed to be okay.

I heard the front door open, and the sound of my family broke through my angst. My husband walked into the room. The sight of him sparked new hope and strength. I reached out to him and said, "Honey, I'm sick. I need a blessing, and then we need to go to the hospital." He gave me a blessing, and then he took me to the emergency room, where they rushed me back for an ultrasound of my abdomen. The technician, who was not supposed to say anything about what she saw, couldn't hide her expression. Yes, it was bad, she whispered. The tears, which hadn't stopped since I'd left my bed, came harder now. I knew what was coming. Five minutes later, we were sitting in my doctor's office. Not an exam room but his real office, with medical books lining the shelves and a plant on his wooden desk. You know, the office you see people taken to in TV shows and movies where they receive bad news. My doctor looked at me from across the desk and said, "Michelle, you have an infection about the size of a dinner plate in your stomach. If we wait any longer to remove it, you will die."

The floor fell out from beneath my feet. *I will die.*

He explained that I'd need another surgery. When? Right now.

I was wheeled upstairs, where I changed and was in the operating room fifteen minutes later. This time I was scared. Terrified. Facing death has a way of doing that. Then I remembered the words from my blessing, that everything would be okay. At that moment, things were definitely not okay. But I realized something as I lay there in that cold, sterile room with beeping monitors, doctors and nurses rushing around me, and a dinner-plate-sized infection trying to kill me—it wasn't over yet. There was still time for it to turn out okay. This wasn't my end. And even if it was the end of my mortal life, I knew there was life after this place. In the end, no matter what happened, I would truly be okay, just like God had said. This realization, on what could have been my deathbed, brought me peace and strength. Faith replaced fear. I *could* do this; I could fight this infection. And God would make sure I was okay because He had a plan.

I awoke a few hours later surrounded by my family. I was still alive. I was okay. After a five-day hospital stay, I was back home again. After a week, I was walking laps around my backyard. A year later, I ran my first 5K race. It truly did turn out okay. There was never a need to be afraid. He knew that, and I believe He tried to tell me in many different ways.

God doesn't want us to be afraid. That is the answer He gave me that stormy day when Paige was sick, as well as in my blessing the night before my first surgery. It is the message God has for all of His children. We need only skim through the scriptures to find His voice.

One night, the disciples of Jesus were in the middle of the sea, in a ship being tossed about by a powerful wind. Jesus approached them walking on the water. When the disciples saw him, they were afraid, but Jesus called out to them, "Be of good cheer; it is I; be not afraid" (Matthew 14:27).

After the Last Supper, Jesus taught His Apostles, instituted the sacrament, and washed their feet. They had been with Him for three years. They had walked with Him, been taught by Him, and had witnessed His miracle. They understood on some level what was to come, but we have little to indicate that on that night they had any understanding of the reality of the Savior's words to them "Let not your heart be troubled, neither let it be afraid" (John 14:27). They did not seem to be burdened with fear for the approaching arrest, torture, and death of their friend and master. In fact, later that evening, as the Savior knelt in the Garden of Gethsemane and suffered beyond our mortal comprehension for us, His Apostles slept under a tree (see Mark 14:37).

Before Jesus died, He told them He would go away (see John 14:28) and to not be afraid. However, when faced with the reality of His prophetic words, they were not only afraid but also filled with sorrow and shock. How could this have happened? And when they heard the glorious news that He had risen once again, they fell to their knees and worshipped him. The first recorded words Christ offered to them were, "Be not afraid" (Matthew 28:10).

Eighteen hundred years later, Jesus Christ shared the same message with His modern-day disciples, "Verily I say unto you my friends, fear not, let your hearts be comforted" (D&C 98:1). Satan wants us to be afraid. Heavenly Father and our Savior do not. So why do They allow us to be afraid? Why can't They simply take fear away from us? Why must we experience it?

I love Sister Virginia Pearce's answer to this question:

> Perhaps our Heavenly Father's greatest hope is that through our fears we may choose to turn to him. The uncertainties of earth life can help to remind each of us that we are dependent on him. But that reminder is not automatic. It involves our agency. We must *choose* to take our fears to him, *choose* to trust him, and *choose* to allow him to direct us. We must make these choices when what we feel most inclined to do is to rely more and more on our own frantic and often disoriented thinking.
>
> As we try to live his commandments and pray to him, there are things he will direct us to do that will help calm our fears. These actions often require great courage and direction from the Holy Ghost. The Holy Ghost may help us to understand when and with whom we should share our fears. He will support us as we face our fears and try to do things we have never done before. (Pearce, "Fear")

In my darkest hour, when I was most afraid, my thoughts turned to God. That is a common reaction. When things are going well, we often overlook His hand in our lives, but when the chips are down and we are facing difficult circumstances, our spirits reach for Him. That's what Heavenly Father wants—for us to reach out to Him, to believe in Him. He wants us to have faith in Him and Jesus Christ, to "be not afraid, only believe" (Mark 5:36). Don't be afraid. Believe. Have faith, because faith is the opposite of fear.

Here is another question to ponder: Is it possible to be afraid and have faith at the same time? Yes and no. They cannot exist in the same exact place, just as light and darkness cannot, but they can exist at the same time. Think of a dark room that welcomes a ray of light. Where the light shines, there is no darkness, but the darkness is still in the same room. Likewise, we can have moments of doubt and fear and still have faith at the same time. The key is to see it not as an either/or situation but as a sliding scale of faith and fear. At different points in our lives, our fear might be greater than our faith, and other times our faith might be greater than our fear. Our great quest is to make our faith greater than our fear until someday only faith exists in us.

In the New Testament, we read of a faithful yet fearful father of a sick child. He brought his son to Jesus's disciples in hopes that they could heal him. This caused a great deal of contention and questioning from the scribes. As Jesus came upon this hostile scene and inquired of the matter, the father of the boy who was suffering from convulsions, foaming at the mouth, and gnashing his teeth approached Him.

"Master, I have brought unto thee my son . . . if thou canst do any thing, have compassion on us, and help us." Jesus answered, "If thou canst believe, all things are possible to him that believeth."

Without hesitation, this father declared his faith. "Lord, I believe." Then in humble acknowledgement, he admitted that along with his belief there was doubt, maybe fear, as well. He immediately pleaded with Jesus, "Help thou mine unbelief" (Mark 9:17, 22–24).

Elder Jeffrey R. Holland so eloquently spoke of the coexistence of faith and fear as he shared this insight on this father's plea. He said, "When facing the challenge of faith, the father asserts his strength first and only then acknowledges his limitation. His initial declaration is affirmative and without hesitation: 'Lord, I believe.' I would say to all who wish for more faith, remember this man! In moments of fear or doubt or troubling times, hold the ground you have already won, even if that ground is limited" (Holland, "Lord, I Believe").

You have faith! You've won some ground! Hold on to it, Elder Holland says, and base your choices not on your fears but on the faith you have. Elder Holland continued:

> In the growth we all have to experience in mortality, the spiritual equivalent of this boy's affliction or this parent's desperation is going to come to all of us. When those moments come and issues surface, the resolution of which is not immediately forthcoming, hold fast to what you already know and stand strong until additional knowledge comes. It was of this very incident, this specific miracle, that Jesus said, "If ye have faith as a grain of mustard seed, ye shall say unto this mountain, Remove hence to yonder place; and it shall remove; and nothing shall be impossible unto you" (Matthew 17:20). The size of your faith or the degree of your knowledge is not the issue—it is the integrity you demonstrate toward the faith you do have and the truth you already know. (Holland, "Lord, I Believe")

Let me repeat his last sentence: "The size of your faith or the degree of your knowledge is not the issue—it is the integrity you demonstrate toward the faith you do have and the truth you already know." How wonderful to know that we can act in faith even if we still feel fear! Your fear may be infinitesimal, or it may be monumental. The faith you have may be as tiny as a mustard seed or as giant as a mountain. What matters is *how* you exercise your faith in the face of fear.

Jesus healed the boy because of the faith-filled plea of his father, *even though* the father had fear and doubt. Despite an open acknowledgment of his struggle, the father chose to bring his son to Jesus. He believed in spite of his fears and doubts. And in the face of them, he *acted* on his belief and in faith turned to the Lord.

Beneath our hopes and fears is the bedrock desire to feel secure and happy and loved. That is just what Heavenly Father wants for us. In the Lord's words, "Be of good cheer, and do not fear, for I the Lord am with you, and will stand by you" (D&C 68:6). He is with us. He loves us. He doesn't plan on leaving our side. He wants us to believe in Him and *believe Him*. He wants us to choose faith over fear and be happy.

Hope, the Sweetest Reason

In most areas of our lives, we have a pretty clear picture of how we want things to be. Whether it comes to our health, our home, our relationships, our jobs, or even our discipleship, we have in our minds what we hope each will look like. That picture creates in our minds a hope of expectations or results that are most pleasing to us. They are what we want to happen, things that *would* happen if we had our way. This spans across the board from external to internal expectations. (We want our children to be well behaved and healthy and make choices that will bring them joy. We want our spouses to treat us with respect, kindness, love, and adoration. We want our homes to be tidy and functional. We want to be successful in our jobs and other endeavors. We want to look and feel our best. We want to be appreciated, valued, and loved. We want to be of worth, to be needed. We want to be happy and have joy.) Most of what we hope for is good. Hope is the sweetest reason that drives us to attain control.

We find no fault in our apparent righteous hopes and expectations because all of these are worthy of hoping and working for. Indeed they are splendid things to desire. Often, in an effort to realize our hopes, we attempt to exercise control over something. We aren't trying to be control freaks. We just want to achieve the optimal picture in our minds of how we think life should be in order for us and others to have the greatest benefit and reward.

In the Book of Mormon, Nephi, the youngest of four brothers, was righteous and unwavering in his faith in God. The Lord had required many sacrifices from Nephi's family. Nephi understood his part and trusted God with the rest. His oft-quoted motto was "I will go and do the things which the Lord hath commanded, for I know that the Lord giveth no commandments unto the children of men, save he shall prepare a way for them that they may accomplish the thing which he commandeth them" (1 Nephi 3:7).

Nephi's two oldest brothers, Laman and Lemuel, were prone to anger and rebellion, which brought much pain to the other family members. Nephi did everything he could to help them. He prayed for them (see 1 Nephi 2:18), talked to them (see 1 Nephi 7:8), encouraged them (see 1 Nephi 16:4, 17:15), and forgave them when they hurt him (see 1 Nephi 7:21), which happened often. Nephi loved his brothers and had "joy and great *hopes* of them" (1 Nephi 16:5; emphasis added). It was this hope, in part, that led Nephi to do everything in his power, or his personal control, to help them. He simply wanted them to be happy.

Hope is a strong motivator for our actions. It is a feel-good, divinely given engine that drives us to do much of what we do. Righteous hope leads to pure faith and action. Paul taught the Hebrews that "faith is the substance of things hoped for" (Hebrews 11:1). It is the *hope* that forgiveness is possible that feeds our decision to believe, then exercise our faith unto the act of repenting. It is our *hope* that we can be saved that fortifies our faith in the Savior.

Righteous hope is optimism in its purity. Our hope that everything will turn out fine in the end—that the good guy always wins, that right will prevail over wrong—is what compels us to keep going in spite of difficult times. We hope God loves us; we hope there is a plan. We hope we have a purpose. We hope what we have been taught is really true. From this hope springs our choice to believe, and from our belief springs the action of faith.

Not all hope is righteous, however. Many have hoped to amass fortunes, obtain fame, and gain personal comfort and worldly success. This hope, dream, or expectation has carried many to positions of power. History is replete with men and women who have aspired to the halls of power only to arrive with scars of corruption and greed. Unrighteous hope does not feed righteous faith. In its extreme, it can lead to action devoid of conscience and care.

What do we want? What do we hope for? What actions are born from our hopes? Do they bring us closer to God's plan for us? Take an honest look inside yourself. What do you really want? What are you really hoping for?

Righteous hope is what keeps us going when everything seems wrong. It compels us to "against hope [believe] in hope" (Romans 4:18). Nephi tells us to "press forward with a steadfastness in Christ, having a perfect brightness of hope" (2 Nephi 31:20). Hope is the thing that keeps our hands reaching when we are tired, keeps us praying through our tears, and keeps us breathing when we don't think we can make it another minute. We do make it, though, because we *hope* we can. Hope is what makes us brave. Hope colors our view, drives our actions, and keeps our eyes pointed toward heaven. Hope is more powerful than fear.

We must use all that God has given us to starve the fear and feed the hope and faith. Trust in Him as He trusts in us. God has hopes for us, expectations for us. He's got big plans, perfect plans. That's what His work and glory is all about (Moses 1:39). It's all about us. As we grab hold and let go of control, we must look to God. For when we do, there's no need to fear, and there's every reason to hope!

Chapter 4

Influence vs. Control

"Blessed is the influence of one true, loving human soul on another."
—Mary Ann Evans (George Eliot)

OUTSIDE OF OURSELVES, WE CANNOT truly control much of anything. In many cases, we *feel* we are controlling what is around us—our weight, our homes, our finances, our spouses, our children—when the reality is we aren't. Now, before you feel completely immobilized and powerless, take heart in the fact that you never have—and you've made it this far!

Controlling every facet of our lives was never in God's plan. He didn't put us here to control each other or the world around us. He placed us here so we could learn to control ourselves and *influence* the world around us for good. We do this through our choices and our character. According to the Googlesphere, *influence* is "the capacity to have an effect on the character, development, or behavior of someone or something, or the effect itself." This means that through our choices, we can have an effect on the condition or outcome of the people and circumstances around us.

We most definitely can influence the realization of our goals as we work toward them. We make plans and preparations, take steps, and work hard to create the kind of life we want. Ultimately, however, any number of external forces can change our plans in a moment's notice. An angry boss can fire you, a disgruntled teacher can fail you, an alarm clock won't go off, or traffic is bad. Far more serious and unexpected events happen in life as well—sickness, natural disasters, crime, even death. These, among others, put an agonizing wrench in our once-solid plans. In most cases, there is nothing we can do to prevent them from occurring. We have no control over them.

We can't control them, nor should we want to. That's not saying we shouldn't want a righteously desired outcome, of course. Having healthy goals, dreams, and expectations is great because it's not the goal but how we get there that is often the problem. For example, your goal may be to make someone smile. You have two options: first, you could try to control them by demanding they smile, or even taking your fingers and physically drawing their downturned lips into the appearance of a grin. Or you could choose to simply smile at them first. Chances are they will smile back. Mission accomplished. And no one was manhandled in the process.

The sooner we realize we cannot control everything, the sooner we can focus on not just our power of influence but the responsibility that comes with our personal influence. When President David O. McKay extended the call to the Quorum of the Twelve Apostles to the young Thomas S. Monson, he offered this counsel: "There is one responsibility that no one can evade. That is the effect of one's personal influence" (Monson, "Your Personal Influence").

You've heard it said, "Be the change you wish to see in the world." Through righteous desires and good works, we can have a powerful influence on our communities, our work, our schools, our churches, our country, and our homes. We can be as a candle shining with good intentions and good works for those around us (see Matthew 5:15–16). If you ever want to test the power of influence, spend an entire day being happy. Happiness is just as contagious as a yawn!

There are so many ways you can influence our world. You can

> influence your health by making wise food choices and exercising as you're able.

> influence your church family by choosing to be compassionate and forgiving, serving and loving.

> influence your workplace by not gossiping and having integrity and keeping a high work ethic.

> influence your finances by saying no to wants and yes to needs as you build up savings and pay off debt.

> influence your schools by volunteering and showing gratitude toward teachers, and if you're a student, by working hard and keeping a positive attitude.

You get the picture. Though we cannot control people or circumstances, our personal influence can make a huge difference in the world around us.

As we move our attention from the outside world to our inner circle, relinquishing the notion of control for influence can be more difficult. We want to feel we have control of our homes and our families, right? I mean, that's our job, isn't it? No. In reality, we can influence them, but we cannot ultimately control them. Sometimes, though, our influence can be so strong that we mistake it for control.

Take a disobedient child, for example, and our parental mantra of "Because I said so." It might seem that we have controlled the child as they stomp off to their bedroom, take the garbage out, do their homework, or whatever else we may have demanded of them, but in reality, the child *chose* to be obedient. We did not force them to. We cannot *make* them obey, though we can surely influence them. With our hands on hips and eyebrows raised, they might feel as if they had no choice but to obey, but ultimately it was our *very strong* influence that persuaded them to choose to comply.

What about others? Have you ever wished your sister would *finally* take your advice because you know what is best for her? Do you ever wish you could have your husband do exactly what you think he should be doing all the time? Are you active in your efforts to get people to do what you want them to be doing, even if that control is born out of good intentions?

You Can't Ride a Dead Horse

I once had an interesting conversation with a newlywed wife. She seemed a cheerful lady, always smiling and laughing. I asked her if she was always that happy. Her response surprised me. She said, "Not when my husband and I are alone. It's hard to be so happy when he has so many things to work on." She went on to explain that she was constantly busy telling him everything he needed to change, from habits to behaviors to the way he showed his love for her. She considered herself a good wife, and she wanted him to be a good husband. She was "helping him"— over and over and over again. She was trying to make him a better husband, and it was exhausting.

I suggested she give him some room to breathe and perhaps focus on her own choices for a while. But in her eyes, that simply wouldn't do. She had to make him change. If she didn't change him, he would continue on the same path and would never improve. Then she would never be happy.

I then said, "Men are like horses."

She looked confused.

"If you ride a horse without letting it rest, it will run until it dies. You need to give the horse a rest."

She still didn't understand.

I went on to explain. "If you constantly barrage your husband with criticism, scolding, and disappointment, you will kill him and your relationship. You cannot force him to be who you want him to be. Just as a horse needs time to rest and recover, your husband needs a rest from criticism and 'helping.' He needs time and space to learn and grow. You need to give him a rest."

She was skeptical. "But what if he doesn't change?"

"What if you don't change?"

"Oh."

The concept that we cannot control those around us can be difficult to grasp. That was the struggle of this young wife and a lesson I needed to learn as a newlywed as well. My story was much the same as hers until a wise person gave me the same advice I gave her. At first I thought, *No way. If I do that, I will become an even better wife and he won't improve at all. That's not fair.* But I took their counsel. I gave him a rest and started to focus on myself.

What I learned was surprising and, initially, a little depressing. When I stopped focusing on him and started to work on myself, I realized I wasn't as good a wife or person as I'd thought I was. I realized I was critical, short-tempered, slow to forgive, and quick to feel sorry for myself. I began to realize how much *I* needed to work on. *So* not what I had expected!

I started focusing my attention on the things I had control of: my choice to love him as he was, how I chose to show my love for him, my reactions, my attitude, my responses. I tried to be the kind of person I knew my Father in Heaven would have me be. As I started to focus on changing myself, a funny thing happened: I began to change . . . and so did my husband.

It is difficult to say if his change came about because I gave him room to grow rather than always "helping." Perhaps, I think more realistically, the appearance of his change came because as I grew, my capacity to love grew; I was able to see him for who he was and not for what I thought he should be. I no longer felt the need to make him act a certain way, or tell me he loved me in a specific way, or clean the kitchen a certain way. I didn't feel the need to force him into being what I wanted, because I realized he already *was* who I wanted—imperfections and all.

The Lord clearly states that we should not "exercise control or dominion or compulsion upon the souls of the children of men, in any degree of unrighteousness." When we do, "the heavens withdraw themselves; the Spirit of the Lord is grieved" (D&C 121:37).

Lucifer's unrighteous desire to compel each of us to always choose the right was enough to disqualify him to become our Savior (see Moses 4:3). So force is not a good thing.

Our individual right to choose is an intrinsic part of Father's plan. Choosing to be like Him is the only way to become like Him. Personal growth, change, and conversion cannot ever be forced. They must be chosen. That is true for ourselves *and* the people around us.

The question may arise: is being compelled the same thing as being forced or controlled? Consider the Zoramites in the Book of Mormon who were "compelled to be humble" by their poor circumstances (Alma 32:13). They were very much forced into their destitute lifestyles due to the pride and greed of their brothers. At that time, they had little to no control over their circumstances, but they had full control over their reactions. They were *influenced* by their circumstances to humility and then faith, not forced. It was their internal condition, not their external circumstances, that pleased Alma because he knew they were prepared to hear the word of God (see Alma 32:6).

Alma taught that we should be "humble, and be submissive and gentle; easy to be entreated; full of patience and long-suffering" (Alma 7:23). Does that sound like control or the seeds of righteous influence? As we keep our focus on the one thing we do have control over—ourselves—others might see the change in us and want to change themselves. They might be easier to love, but so will we.

When we stand before our Savior to be judged, we won't be standing next to anyone else—not our spouse, our parents, our children, our friends. And He will want to know how we did, who we became, and what we did to follow Him. We cannot say, "Well, I tried to change, but Harvey just had so much to work on. I was so busy helping him that I didn't have any time to work on myself." We will be held accountable for ourselves, no one else. That means we can't blame anyone else either.

It is a scary thing to do, to change our focus from someone else back to ourselves, to give up that false sense of control. But we will change and grow. We will also inspire and influence others to change and grow.

The (Un)happy Homemaker

It is easy to grasp the idea that we cannot control the economy, the weather, politics, or the environment, but we may wonder, can we have control over the things closer to us, like our homes? That answer, to the dismay of many a mother and homemaker, is no. No matter what we do, new dust falls, dishes are dirtied, and the home is lived in. We can surely *influence* the appearance by vacuuming and cleaning. We can snap at the kids for leaving toys on the floor and have guests take their shoes off at the door, all in an effort to try to fit our homes into our ideal picture, but eventually it will get dirty again.

During my oophorectomy hospital stay, I left my husband home for a week with two toddlers. Like many dads, he started the week with, "No problem. How hard can this be?" I'll never forget their visit on about day five. My then-three-year-old Paige showed up with a mullet on the left side of her head, thanks to some unsupervised experimentation with scissors. My husband looked frazzled as he replayed the events of the day. Then, in exasperation, he said, "Do you realize how much time I spend a day just picking up socks off the floor?" I laughed, even though it hurt my stomach to do it. Yes, I did! Socks, toys, wrappers, books, shoes, blankets, homework, chips. Children are a boatload of joy, but they leave a wake of destruction behind them.

It took me a while to give up the dream of trying to control everything and everyone in my home. It was hard because I saw my home as a direct reflection of me. There is some truth to that, but what I forgot is that it isn't just me living in it. I'm sharing those four walls with four other people who each has their own idea of clean and tidy. I've done all I can to have a spotless, seamlessly running home. I've made chore charts, delivered consequences, gotten upset with my kids, done their chores for them because sometimes it was just easier, and found myself mad that my house didn't look like I thought it should.

My efforts to make a perfect home have driven me to emit such a negative influence that the feeling in my house hasn't been perfect at all. In those instances, it wasn't even good! I knew I needed to change. I got to the point where I made my chore charts, *influenced* my children with natural consequences, and let things be what they were. I stopped crying over spilled milk. I could influence it but couldn't control it. And once I let that idea of control go, once I allowed the kids to not put their shoes away every time or let the house get cluttered because we had other family stuff going, *I* lightened up. I was happier, and in turn, my influence was more positive. I'm not ready to cross-stitch "A Touch of Clutter Makes for a Happy Mom," but there is a bit of truth to it.

This doesn't mean we should let our house go, just like we don't stop bathing because we get dirty during the day. But as we see our efforts for what they are—an attempt to *influence* the condition of our home, not a quest to control it—we can find peace in a little clutter. We can have happy moments as we cuddle with our children on a pile of warm, unfolded laundry. We can let the dinner dishes sit while we go on a date with our spouse. We will find time to pursue other righteous endeavors as we let the legend of an always-spotless house go.

Speaking of Children . . .

Speaking of children . . . wouldn't it be great if we could control them? I used to think so. Their lives would be so much easier if they did exactly what we told them to all the time, right? But then I was reminded that that was the adversary's plan from the beginning. He wanted to take away man's agency and force us to always choose the right, even if we didn't want to. That is not how character is built or how potential is reached. Not for us or our children.

As stated before, fear and hope for our children can compel us to try to control them, and part of our motivation is selfishness and personal preference. My youngest daughter loves to drum. She doesn't have a drum set though, so she smacks everything around her. The kitchen counter. The couch. The back of my seat in the van. I must be getting old and crotchety because the sound of smacking grates on my nerves. When she does it, I want it to stop, so I tell her to. Not because I have any hope or fear for her future or safety but simply because I don't want to hear it. If I were more generous, I'd probably buy her a drum set. But for now, I am trying to ease up on my control and let her drum away and enjoy it because she loves it. Even if it makes me want to pound my head into the wall.

The best thing we can do for our children isn't to control them but to teach them truth. Teach them the principles of the gospel of Jesus Christ, including self-control, and provide a safe place for them to practice what they are learning. The wife of a US general, after admiring the conduct of young members of the Church, asked President Packer, "Tell me, how [are you] able to control your youth and build such character as we have seen in your young men?"

His reply is as much about heavenly parenting as it is about earthly parenting. He said, "We develop control by teaching freedom." The control of which he spoke, however, was not of the adult's control over the children but of the control the children learn to have over themselves. He went on to say, "There is an obedience that comes from a knowledge of the truth that transcends any external form of control. We are not obedient because we are blind, we are obedient because we can see" (Packer, "Agency and Control").

It is our job as parents to teach our children right and wrong and help them see their own ability to choose. When asked how one person could govern so many people, Joseph Smith replied, "I teach them correct principles, and they govern themselves" (*Teachings of Presidents of the Church: Joseph Smith*). We are to teach our children the gospel of Jesus Christ, the power of agency, and the principles of accountability and responsibility.

Just as fear and faith coexist on a sliding scale, so do dependence and independence as children grow from helpless newborn babes to capable adults. They are not accessories that adorn our lives or trophies that show how well we parent. It is not our job to dress them up and show them off, control them, and manipulate them. We must teach them from the time they are young that God loves them and that they have the power to choose right from wrong.

We must teach them that though they can choose whatever they may, they cannot choose the consequences and effects of their influence. That is a lot for our children to understand all at once. The finesse of parenting is in the art of handing learning over to them line upon line, a nugget of information here, a responsibility there, knowing how and when to give independence and knowledge. In today's world, children have easy access to all kinds of information and experiences that their maturity, spirituality, and intellect simply aren't ready for. As parents, it's our responsibility to protect them from that which is simply too heavy for them to understand.

In her book *The Hiding Place*, Corrie ten Boom tells of a time when she asked her father, an early twentieth-century Dutch watchmaker, the meaning of *sexsin*. She said,

> He turned to look at me, as he always did when answering a question, but to my surprise he said nothing. At last he stood up, lifted his traveling case from the rack over our heads, and set it on the floor.
>
> "Will you carry it off the train, Corrie?" he said.
>
> I stood up and tugged at it. It was crammed with the watches and spare parts he had purchased that morning.
>
> "It's too heavy," I said.
>
> "Yes," he said. "And it would be a pretty poor father who would ask his little girl to carry such a load. It's the same way, Corrie, with knowledge. Some knowledge is too heavy for children. When you are older and stronger you can bear it. For now you must trust me to carry it for you."
>
> And I was satisfied. More than satisfied— wonderfully at peace.

> There were answers to this and all my hard
> questions—for now I was content to leave them
> in my father's keeping. (29)

We are our children's keepers—keepers of knowledge, faith, strength, experience, and opportunity. We set boundaries, dole out discipline (with the intent to teach, not punish), teach them to work hard, love them, and give them opportunities to become the adults we hope they will be.

The gospel of Jesus Christ offers our children peace, direction, strength, purpose, and growth. Jesus Christ quoted the prophet Isaiah, "And all thy children shall be taught of the Lord; and great shall be the peace of thy children" (3 Nephi 22:13). Nowhere does the Savior speak of controlling our children. In fact, He tells us that we need to "become as little children," or else "ye shall not enter into the kingdom of heaven. Whosoever therefore shall humble himself as this little child, the same is greatest in the kingdom of heaven" (Matthew 18:3–4).

Parenting is hard. Kids are hard to raise. Even though we understand the perfect principles of parenting, we are still imperfect, and we *will* mess up. Many of my most fervent prayers regarding my children are, "God, please fix what I broke today." I am selfish and impatient and have been tired since 1996 when I was put on bedrest during my pregnancy with my oldest. I am amazed at how many times I can tell my children to not leave their shoes in the middle of the floor and have them still do it anyway. Every. Day. I have to remind them to do their homework, brush their teeth, eat their vegetables, not watch too much TV, get good grades. My work is *never* done! I find myself yelling, "If you would just do exactly what I say all the time, my life would be so much easier!" As if it is all about me.

How grateful I am for a Heavenly Father with infinite patience! He has every reason to throw His hands up in the air and say, "You know what? I'm done. You never listen, and you never will." But He doesn't. He is the perfect and ultimate example of a parent. He is always there, not controlling me but *influencing* me with

His Spirit, with people He's placed in my path, with the Light of Christ, and with so many other divine means.

He is not only my Father in Heaven, but He is also *my children's* Father in Heaven. He helps me be the parent they need while they are in my home. And as they get older and leave the safety of home, I entrust them to His care. I know I shouldn't be afraid, but there is a part of me that longs to keep them with me, as if I am the best person for the job. It is much like the feeling I had when the labor and delivery nurses came in to take my hours-old firstborn out of the room for testing. "No," I told them. They could do it there. He was not to leave my side. I didn't care who they were, nursing degrees or not; *I* was his mother, and *I* knew what was best for him. But I didn't and still don't. God does, and I will have to entrust my children to Him.

As we get older, our children will leave the nest and pave their own ways. They may make decisions contrary to what we would have for them. They might go down paths that lead to heartache and pain. As a parent, I can imagine it would be unbearable to watch. We want to shake them and make them choose right! But just as we have our agency, they do too. All we can do is teach them the best we can, pray for them, love them, and trust that God is watching over them and loving them far more greatly and deeply than we do.

There is a verse in Proverbs that says, "Train up a child in the way he should go: and when he is old, he will not depart from it" (Proverbs 22:6). It is a beautiful promise, one that I will count on. I will do my best not to control my child but to train him in righteousness. As he grows, I will trust him to make his own decisions, and if his differ from the ones I would have made for him or that God would have made for him, I will find peace in the fact that someday, when he is old, he might return once again.

It is the promise brought to life by the Prodigal Son (Luke 15:11–32) and by our own lives. How many of us have made choices contrary to our Heavenly Father's will? How many of us have made decisions and mistakes that have brought heartache and sorrow into our lives and perhaps the lives of others? And yet, here we are, trying to continue to learn and grow, repent and improve—to return to Him. Do not our earthly children deserve the same hope and opportunity that God gives His heavenly children? The answer is a resounding yes. And that is found in love, not control.

So Now What?

Once we accept that total control of the world and people around us is a myth, we open our hearts to accept the truth that we can control only ourselves and that God has the rest. And as we claim personal control and give the rest to God, we begin to see more clearly our responsibility and our accountability. We begin to trust God's plan for all of us and for each of us. As we come to do that, our ability to righteously influence the people in our lives and the world around us will not only be good but can also be monumental in our homes, our communities, or even a bouncy house. We can have peace and joy in a balanced life.

PART TWO:

Giving the Rest to God

Chapter 5
Let Go of Control. Give it Back to God

"Trust in the Lord with all thine heart; and lean not unto thine own understanding."

—Proverbs 3:5

The Old Country Road

Now that we have a pretty clear picture of what we can control, let's move on to what we can't control: everything else. Terrifying? Frustrating? Sometimes very much so. Go back to the imagery of Paige's dream: we can decide to put on high heels with the intent of going to the opera, but what do we do when we end up in the bouncy house? What then? What do we do when we are prepared to go one way and life takes us down an entirely different path?

There is a lovely old country road not far from my home. It is one of my favorite drives. The scenery is beautiful. It twists and turns past pastures, farms, homes, and trees. When we first moved to the area, I decided to take the road home after running some errands. This was pretty daring in the pre-GPS days. But even though I wasn't familiar with its course, I knew that if I stayed on the road, it would lead me back home.

After driving a few windy miles, I looked ahead to see the road stretch far in front of me. With its curves and bends, it was nice to finally get a clear picture of where I was going.

And then something very strange happened as I reached the top of a small hill. My route changed before my eyes. I realized the road that stretched out into the distance was not a part of my path at all! My little country road veered sharply to the left.

Even though the new direction was unexpected, I stayed on my country road and eventually made it home.

Since then, I have driven that road a thousand times. I think about that experience nearly every time I drive it. Like this road, life has its twists and turns, its hills and beautiful scenery. But we can be sure that if we are on the right road, we are headed home, even if the path home doesn't always take us where we think it will.

For example, as I mentioned at the beginning of this book, I planned on having a big family—five children. That was the magic number. I knew having a big family was His will for me. After all, it was a good and righteous goal, right? Well, my road took some unexpected turns full of heartache and faith. Two of my children came to us the traditional way, but after many years, our third came His way—through adoption. From the turns and hills I hadn't seen or expected.

Heavenly Father really does have control of the rest. He has a road for each of us to take. I believe He takes great care in leading and guiding us down that road back to Him. On our own road in life, we may have times where we look around and think, "This is not where I thought I would be." We might have great goals and big dreams and think we know exactly what makes us happy where we are going, but then something changes. We may have unexpected tragedies or trials, heartbreak or misfortune. We may look ahead and see no happy ending.

Take heart. Though the experiences are real and necessary for our growth, they are not the destination. They are merely turns in our road.

Your Father in Heaven knows us better than we know ourselves. He knows what will truly bring us the greatest joy, and oftentimes it is not what we had planned. We could fight His will, choose to be angry with Him, drive recklessly, or even turn off the road. Or we can choose to believe in Him and trust in His plan and enjoy the ride.

Remember the group of believers I spoke of in chapter two? Even during their life of suffering and bondage, they "[bore] up their burdens with ease, and they did submit cheerfully and with patience to all the will of the Lord" (Mosiah 24:15). What made them so cheerful in the middle of their afflictions, when their road led them in a completely different direction? It was their willingness to recognize and trust in God's will. They *chose* to have a positive attitude because they trusted and had faith in the Lord. They had *perspective*. They knew He had a plan and that His plan was better for them in the end than any plan they could think of.

The reward for their faith, their attitude, and their patience was their eventual freedom from that bondage. Through divine intervention, they escaped their bonds and were led to the land of people who received them "with joy" (Mosiah 24:25). Though there were some painful and even unwanted turns in their road, they stayed on the path, obeyed His will, and were led to a better place.

Obey Who?

One of the keys to following God's will, path, or road is obedience. Through obedience we can go where He wants us to go and become who He knows we can become. President Spencer W. Kimball said, "We must learn to master ourselves, by obedience to the Lord's . . . laws . . . so that the hidden things of the spirit may come to us and we attain perfection with the Father and the Son" (Kimball, *Faith Precedes the Miracle*, 280).

But the word *obedience* carries with it a negative connotation to some.

Our family loves to sit together each Sunday night and watch *America's Funniest Home Videos*. We laugh, sometimes until we cry. Years ago, one particular wedding video sent me to the floor. While the couple was taking out their vows, the preacher stated a vow, and the bride repeated it. It went something like this:

"To love."

"To love," the bride said as she tenderly smiled at her husband.

"To cherish."

"To cherish," the bride said with budding tears in her eyes.

"And to obey."

Her head whipped around to the preacher, and her face contorted with surprise. The sweet expressions of love and cherishing were quickly replaced with a look that can only be described as "Obey? I don't think so!"

I laughed pretty hard. My husband laughed even harder. The call to obey her husband struck something deep within her—and it wasn't good.

But that's what we're taught, isn't it? Obey. Submit. In Ephesians, Paul taught, "Wives, submit yourselves unto your own husbands, as unto the Lord" (Ephesians 5:22). So does this mean that to be a good wife and an obedient disciple of Jesus, I must submit my will to my husband and obey him in all things? Yes . . . and no.

When I was first married, in my efforts to be a good wife, I tried to treat my husband like the head of the household, letting him have the final say in the decisions and trying my best to support him, because I thought that was what I was supposed to do.

During our second year of marriage, we were living in a small apartment. My husband and I shared our room with our infant son. One night the little baby just wouldn't go to sleep. I changed him, fed him, burped him, rocked him, and sang to him. I tried everything, but he refused to be soothed. By this time, he was crying out of sheer exhaustion. He simply didn't want to go to sleep. So I laid him in his crib next to our bed, hoping he would finally grasp the idea it was bedtime. I lay next to my husband, who had been trying to fall asleep in the chaos, as I tried to consider what to do next.

Suddenly my husband jumped out of bed and said, "That's it. I'm putting him in his car seat in the bathroom so we can get some sleep!" He stomped around the end of the bed on his way to the crib but met me instead. I looked him square in the face and said in a low, deep tone, "You will not touch that baby. Go back to bed."

My bold move caught him off-guard and defused any frustration he had had. He sheepishly turned around, bowed his head, and crawled back into bed. I wasn't worried about my husband hurting our son, but I knew putting him in the bathroom was not right and that my husband was only reacting out of exhaustion and frustration. Did I submit to my husband that night? No. Did I obey him? No. Was I wrong? No way.

People tend to associate the word *obey* with a loss of their own will—you do what someone else says regardless of your own will. It is the same thing with *submit*. The word awakens the fear of losing your ground, your will, your freedom.

If you associate these definitions and emotions—fear, loss, no choice—with the words *obey* and *submit*, it is natural to see why the bride pulled back when she was asked to obey her husband-to-be. Who wants to lose the right to live the way they choose? Who wants to be ruled over and subjected to someone else's will and whim, whether to a spouse or even to God?

I've asked myself that question in the past and have admittedly struggled to find an answer that sits well with me. I have a pride issue I'm working on, so I don't like to be told what to do a lot. (I never claimed to be perfect. I'm just trying to learn and share perfect principles.) But as I've pondered the idea of obedience over the years, this is what I've come up with. In the thesaurus, there are many synonyms for the word *submit*: *surrender, give in, yield, accept, succumb*—all of which can carry with them negative undertones. If you do the same search for *obey*, you find *mind, do as you are told, follow, comply with, observe, abide by,* and *conform*.

In the lists of words akin to *submit* and *obey*, there are two phrases listed that I feel speak to what Paul was trying to say: *agree to* and *act upon*. When most people get married, they do it with the intent on staying married. In my marriage to my husband, it is not required to obey each other. But we *are* obligated by our own promises to work in agreement—agree to—with each other toward a shared goal—a healthy, eternal relationship. And we should take the appropriate actions—act upon—to ensure we each do our necessary parts. But for it to work, we must have the same goal and work *together*—agree to and act upon.

As my husband submits himself to and agrees with the Lord and acts upon His will for him, whatever my husband asks of me is what the Lord would have me do. I am not below or behind him, taking orders and obeying him. I do not wait for his permission or stamp of approval. I am by his side, agreeing with him *and* the Lord as we both act upon our values and promises together.

If the goals we have agreed to are to speak kindly and respectfully to each other, I will call him on it when he is grouchy and speaks reactively. In addition, if the goals we have agreed upon are to get us out of debt, and I experience a moment of weakness and want to purchase my third purse that month, he calls me on it. He does not deny me the act of buying the purse, but he does remind me of our shared goal and my part in acting upon that goal. We keep each in check because we both want this marriage to last.

If looked at in the clearer light of the gospel, we see that husband and wife have different roles but stand as equals. Obeying and submitting, agreeing to and acting upon the principles of the gospel and all that is good and right. We are together in one righteous purpose.

Submit and *obey*. If we could get rid of the negative connotations of these words and our own personal baggage, we would see them for what they truly mean—especially in the light of our relationship with Heavenly Father. *Agree to* and *act upon*. I submit to the will of the Lord. That doesn't mean I lie down like a doormat and let whatever happens happen. It means I *agree* to allow the Lord to have the power to direct my life—and who better to direct it than the One who created it and knows all? I *choose* to obey the commandments of the Lord. That doesn't mean I am bitter and resentful because of all the rules and restrictions He puts upon me. It means I willingly act upon the directions and requirements the Lord has given me in His wise knowledge and purposes.

When properly (that being the key word) exercised, to submit and obey are keys to a healthy, reciprocal relationship with Father in Heaven. Humility is the key to understanding and doing these two things. Submit and obey. Agree to and act upon.

Do I submit to and obey my husband now? Yes. Does he submit to and obey me? Of course. We agree with each other's goals and actions. Together, we act upon the principles and values we share. We are equals in every way.

Do I submit to and obey my Father in Heaven? Of course. Does He, in turn, lead me down the road that's right for me? I'm counting on it. I believe He wants to give me all that He has, if only I choose to give my will to Him—make Him my priority, strive to be like Him in my actions and reactions, choose to cheerfully follow Him, and believe in Him as best I can.

Letting Go

In speaking of control, people often say they are "letting go of control" or "giving it back to God." But the reality is, most of what we are letting go of or giving back was never ours to begin with. By letting go of control, we are simply admitting to ourselves and to Him that we never had it in the first place. Only when we give our will to God do we allow Him to orchestrate our lives and direct us down the road He has prepared. Our lives can transform from one person letting life happen to them to a divine team of purpose and power. How can we do that? Just how do we let go of trying to control everything else and seek to live and accept God's will for us? I propose the following five steps:

Rely on faith

Reach for and receive personal revelation

Refocus

Relinquish your desires for His

Remember

As we follow these steps, we can learn how to let go, give the control back to God, learn His will, and follow it.

Rely on Faith

The first, and perhaps most important, thing to understand and believe is that Heavenly Father loves us and wants what is ultimately best for us. The key word in that sentence is *ultimately*. Some, if not much, of what we are allowed to experience in life may not appear to have any reason other than to torture and torment us. But when we understand God is in charge, and if we are doing all we can to claim our personal (righteous) control, anything and everything He allows us to experience can be consecrated for our ultimate good if we allow it (see 2 Nephi 2:2).

I have an issue with elevators. My issue is real, though it doesn't keep me from using them. I am not afraid of them. I simply don't like them—especially when they call me fat. Or when they try to kill me. It's still undecided which is worse. A few years back, I was on an errand to pick up some medicine at the local hospital pharmacy. I parked on the second floor of the parking garage, leaving me two options to reach the third-floor hospital entrance: the stairs or the elevator. The stairs were obviously the more active and healthy route, making them the logical choice, but I opted for the elevator instead. I wasn't feeling very inspired to run stairs after a lunch of a juicy hamburger and all-you-can-eat garlic fries.

Though the pharmacy was only one floor above, you wouldn't have thought the elevator knew it. The doors closed slowly, and the elevator growled as if it was annoyed by my presence. It bumped and thumped for five seconds, then ten. Time slowed as my breathing sped up. A giant Ferris wheel of fears circulated in my mind. What if the cables snapped and I crashed to my death? What if the doors jammed and I was stuck for weeks, slowly dying of dehydration and starvation? What if I never saw my family again? What if I died here in this stupid elevator?

For a moment, I felt completely helpless, hopeless, and upset with myself. I had willingly put myself in this situation, into this cold, steel portal to the third-floor pharmacy. It had now become a ticket to my demise. Why hadn't I just walked up the stairs? I could have used the exercise. What had I been thinking?

Then I realized I hadn't been thinking. When presented with the two options, my eyes had been drawn to the glowing elevator button that promised an easy ride. The shiny doors had opened to a clean and inviting elevator. It had been a no-brainer. Why take the stairs when I could ride up in style? I mean, it was one story up. What could happen?

I thought about the ease of the elevator ride, not once giving any thought to the condition of the cables holding the elevator up and pulling it down. I didn't wonder about the last time these cables had been inspected or tested. They were out of sight and out of mind—until my smooth, five-second ride turned into thirty seconds of terror. I stared at the ceiling of my tomb of doom as if my Super Woman X-ray vision would kick in any time and allow me to see through to threadbare cables. No luck. All I could do was take a deep breath, pray, and choose to trust that the cables I couldn't see remained strong.

It occurred to me then that this was a parallel of life. Oftentimes we make choices that seem so effortlessly logical and appealing: marriage, school, kids, career—life. We see glowing buttons that promise us success, happiness, fulfillment, and joy. Shiny doors open to reveal romantic proposals, precious newborn babies, first-day-on-the-job butterflies.

Then the bumps start, and you think, "What in the world did I get myself into?" Marriage is hard work—not the constant lovesick twitterpation you see on TV. That beautiful baby made you gain sixty pounds and is throwing up on you, pooping out food faster than you can get it in him, and crying all night. The job you once loved is now coupled with the politics of difficult coworkers. Life is just not what you expected when you saw the shiny buttons not too long ago—not at all like you'd imagined it to be.

But when the ride you are on starts to bump and thump and life is difficult, consider what is holding you up, what you can't see beyond the ceiling of your life—the hidden cables. Who is keeping you from falling to your demise? Heavenly Father and

Jesus Christ. We can't see them—but we can trust They are there and They know where They are taking us.

After *thirty long seconds*, the elevator opened at the third floor. There might have been a small part of me that was so relieved I could have fallen to the ground and kissed it. But that is really gross, so I didn't. Instead, I casually made my way to the pharmacy to fulfill my errand. On my way back to the third-floor entrance, I faced a choice: do I take the stairs or take a chance on the elevator? I smiled and pushed the glowing button once again. Not just because I didn't want to walk down a flight of stairs, but because this second trip in the elevator represented something more to me—a purposeful act of faith, of walking into the dark just beyond sight, of trusting something I couldn't see or control.

I've heard it said that seeing isn't believing, but believing is seeing. I couldn't agree more. Faith is making the choice to trust that which we cannot see. I couldn't see the cables, but I chose to trust they would not fail me. And they didn't. Neither will our Father in Heaven and our Savior fail us.

As we choose to put our faith in Them—give the control to Them—They will see that we make it to our destinations safely. President Packer said, "Faith, to be faith, must center around something that is not known. Faith, to be faith, must go beyond that for which there is confirming evidence. Faith, to be faith, must go into the unknown. Faith, to be faith, must walk to the edge of the light, and then a few steps into the darkness" (Packer, "What Is Faith?"). It is our faith in God and His plan that gives us the power to move forward in difficult times, past the twists, turns, and bumps of life to our ultimate destination. Indeed, this must be what President Monson meant when he said, "There will be nothing in this world that can defeat us. My beloved brothers and sisters, fear not. Be of good cheer. The future is as bright as your faith" (Monson, "Be of Good Cheer").

But what do we do if our faith is not strong? Heed this inspired advice: "First and forever fan the flame of your faith, because all things are possible to them that believe" (Holland, "Lord, I

Believe"). Your faith doesn't have to be strong to be faith. Rely on the faith you do have, and as you act upon that faith, it will grow. Fan its flames, and let it light your way. Yes, in life there will be bumps and groans, and we'll probably be on a different timeline than we imagined, but it's my guess that when we reach the end, we will find that it was worth every bump and thump to get where God wants us to go.

Reach for and Receive Personal Revelation

Personal revelation is how God speaks to us. It's wonderful to ask Him for direction, but we need to be trying and be willing to hear it as well.

Some friends and I attended a wonderful event for women where we spent a day and a half soaking up the words and music of inspirational presenters and performers. With nearly two thousand women in attendance, we were lucky enough to finagle seats in the front row. I loved being so close to the stage and the people who moved me. My eyes were fixed on the people on the stage in front of me. I listened to every word and song, and my cup was filled.

After we returned home, one of my friends and I were talking about our experience and how much we enjoyed ourselves. She told me something fascinating about one of the presenters who had been sitting near us while another was on the stage. Her name is Kris Belcher, and she is blind. She sat feet from the stage alongside the other presenters, but one thing was different about her. She wasn't facing the presenter giving the message like everyone else. Her head was turned toward the large speaker to the left of the stage. She wasn't focused on where the speaker was but, rather, on where the message was coming from.

Goose bumps riddled my arms and neck as the picture of this amazing woman filled my mind. I couldn't help but see the spiritual correlation. She couldn't see the person talking due to her physical blindness, so she turned to the source of the voice. She faced the speakers because *through the speakers* came the words of those she wanted to hear.

While we are on this earth, we don't have the luxury of seeing our Heavenly Father with our own eyes. Our eyes are, in that way, spiritually blind. However, though we cannot see Him, He has provided a way for us to hear Him through His speaker, the Holy Ghost. Through the Holy Ghost, or the Spirit, God can communicate with us. What a wonderful gift that is! So many are searching for God in this life, wanting badly to see Him, but they feel as though they cannot find Him when all they have to do is turn to the Spirit. When we are focused on the source of His words and the Spirit, we can receive personal revelation.

I want to take a moment to explore just how incredible the phrase "personal revelation" is. A definition of *revelation* is "to make something known in a dramatic or special way, to uncover or bring to light truth and/or understanding." That, in and of itself, is pretty awesome. Personal revelation is when we are given direct knowledge, thoughts, feelings, or impressions from God. Think about that for a moment. Through the Holy Ghost, the God of all that is great and small has the power to impart His wisdom to us directly. Him to us.

The Holy Ghost is the one who turns our prayers and thoughts from monologues into conversations. God can and does communicate with each of His children. He reaches past our doubts and fears and weaknesses and inabilities into our souls. Through the Spirit, we are taught new things, and we remember old things (see John 14:26). We receive comfort and truth (John 15:26). We are given answers and direction directly from the One who knows all.

God speaks to His children individually and intently. What a supremely divine and loving truth that is! To know when we have a question we can ask Heavenly Father, and if we ask with real intent, having faith, the answers can be made known to us through the Holy Ghost (see Moroni 10:4). Personal revelation is key in turning our will to His because that is *how* we find out His will for us.

Figuring out His will for us can be hard when there is so much going on in our lives. When I send my husband to the store, he is pretty good at getting what I ask for. However, invariably, he also brings home a cornucopia of other unauthorized goodies that appealed to him during his shopping trip. To help him stay on target, I often send him with a written list on a sticky note or a text to ensure he gets what *I* want and need him to get—important items like necessary ingredients for meals and lots of chocolate. Of course, I can't get too mad at him when he rolls in with three extra bags of groceries. I've been known to do the same thing on occasion. I can't tell you how many times I have gone to the store for a list of three things, realized I've forgotten my list, and left with two dozen delicious but so-not-needed treats. The grocery store holds an enticing and distracting bounty of baked goods and frozen desserts. It can be difficult to pass by what looks good to me at that moment while I search for what I *should* be getting.

Life is full of all sorts of enticing and distracting choices and opportunities. It can be easy to go about our lives, grabbing at what looks good to us at the moment while missing what we should really be laying hold of. That's where personal revelation comes in. When we turn our attention to hearing the promptings of the Holy Ghost, we can find out what is on Heavenly Father's list for us. We can be led to those opportunities, experiences, people, and places we might not have considered and also be steered away from what may seem good but ultimately is not for us.

I learned this lesson while driving to church one morning. As I pulled off onto a small two-lane road, I approached a crosswalk where an older man hunched over with a cane in hand waited to cross the street. I slowed down—as a responsible citizen should—preparing to stop my van to let him cross when I heard a voice inside me say, "Do not stop." That didn't make sense. Not only would it be rude, but it would be potentially be unsafe as well. He was a little old man. It was the polite, safe, and logical thing to stop. It would be wrong not to. So I slowed down.

Again I heard the words, "Do not stop."

I pushed the little voice aside, thinking it was just a silly thought. I stopped and smiled at the little old man, who, seeing I had stopped, shuffled slowly in front of my car. Then I looked beyond him to the opposite lane. A large white truck tore around the corner and was barreling down the road toward the crosswalk—and the man! I sat up in my car and grabbed my steering wheel, watching the truck. It showed no signs of stopping. I yelled and waved to warn the man, but he did not see me. He was watching the ground as he shuffled along the painted lines. It appeared he neither saw nor heard the truck racing towards him.

It all happened in just seconds—not even time enough for me to get out of my car and help him. I gasped. A look of horror swept across the driver's face as he realized what was in front of him. He slammed on his brakes and swerved, barely missing the elderly man, who simply waved his cane and smiled as if to say, "Thank you for not hitting me," before continuing on his way across the street.

The truck driver drove past me with his head bowed in embarrassment. Me—I just sat in my stopped car in awe of what had just happened. That man had almost been killed right before my eyes. Then the voice again came to me. This time it said, "I told you not to stop. Next time listen."

The reality of what had just happened and what *could* have happened sank deep into my soul. That little voice I'd heard was an impression from my Father in Heaven—personal revelation through the Holy Ghost—and I had disregarded it. I had doubted it. It hadn't made sense. I'd thought *I* knew better. It was then that I realized it wasn't the driver of the truck who had almost killed that frail, sweet man today. It had been me. If I had followed the impression I had felt and not stopped, that good man would have still been waiting safely on the sidewalk when the truck had barreled down the street. He would have been kept out of harm's way—if only I would have followed that voice.

When the Spirit speaks, even if it doesn't seem logical, listen. When the prompting comes from Heavenly Father, through the Holy Ghost, follow it, even if it doesn't seem important. When the Spirit testifies of truth, even if it doesn't seem believable, believe it.

God is patient with me. He always will be—it's a byproduct of His being a perfect being. I am grateful for that. He spoke. I ignored. He gently reprimanded. I repented. He taught a lesson. I learned.

He is counting on us to learn and grow, to make the correct choices because we choose to, not because we are told to. We should seek out His will and strive to do what He would have us do. In this way, we can make sure we are getting everything in *His* list for us. And when He does speak to us—when something is *so* important that the heavens are parted and the Holy Ghost whispers to our souls words of truth and direction—we should listen and follow. Even if it is as big as mending a broken relationship, repenting, starting over, surviving a trial, giving up a bad habit, or changing our lives for the better, or even something as small as making a phone call, giving a hug, saying a prayer . . . or not stopping at a cross walk. Reach for and receive revelation. Then follow it.

Refocus

A few years ago, my husband and son were gone for a week on a Scouting campout. During the day I was all right, but nighttime proved to be a challenge for me. I had done well that particular week, going to bed at a reasonable hour and not letting my imagination get the best of me, until the third night. I finished watching a movie—one of those girly cry-movies I save for when my husband is gone—and crawled into bed. I looked at the clock. It was 3:00 a.m. and I still wasn't tired, so I pulled out my journal.

As I wrote about my day, a sinister figure in the unlit hallway just outside my door caught the corner of my eye. I put my journal down and squinted through the darkened doorway, unable to see beyond my well-lit room. Convincing myself it was nothing I returned to writing. Then a noise from the dark hallway pulled my attention back. It sounded like it was right outside my door. My heart rate rose, but again I told myself it was nothing. I would be fine if I would just quit looking out there and remained focused on me and my well-lit room. Thump. My eyes darted to the door again. I still couldn't see anything, but the possibility of something real in my hallway became undeniable. Still, I chose to ignore the noise (as if ignoring it would make it less real) and finished writing. Finally, I put my journal away and sank deep into my bed. I pulled the covers up to my chin and glanced at the doorway once more, still not able to see the dark hallway. It must have been my imagination, right?

Soon sleep began to overtake me and my fears. I said my prayers and turned off my bedside lamp. With my bedroom now dark I suddenly realized I could see into hallway, which was lit by the natural light of the moon. To my great relief, there was nothing there.

I stared through my dark room into the lit hallway; I chided myself for being afraid of nothing. It may seem a silly story, but it's analogous to life. When my room was fully lit, it overpowered the natural light in the hallway, and I was unable to see beyond my own room. But when I turned my own light off, I could see what was beyond me. The light in the hallway hadn't changed, but my ability to see the hallway had. In life, what we shine our light or attention on tends to keep us from seeing what is real. When our own needs, wants, desires, disappointments, and frustrations are illuminated in our minds, it becomes infinitely more difficult to see what Heavenly Father has in store. But as we change our focus from our issues, we will see beyond our own will. We will be able to see His hand in our lives, His purposes, and more. Our fears of what *could* be out there are replaced with the peace of knowing He is there.

Where we choose to place our attention and focus will determine what we want and what we will do. It is good to have righteous goals and plans, but when these are illuminated and driven by our own will, it can become difficult to see what might lie beyond them. Especially when the things we work so hard for don't happen the way we want. Our lack of ability to control the desired outcome of a person, thing, or circumstance can welcome fear, anger, resentment, or frustration. These feelings can blur our vision, often leaving us unable to see a greater purpose or plan. What we focus on determines what we see.

After the Savior was crucified and resurrected, He visited the people in the Americas. In the time leading up to His appearance, the land was torn apart by earthquakes, fire, whirlwinds, and all manner of terrifying natural forces. A thick darkness then covered the land, and only the sounds of mourning and loss could be heard. Then a large group of believers gathered at the temple. As they talked with one another about all that had happened, they heard a voice. It wasn't loud or harsh but small and piercing. Though they heard it, they couldn't understand it. The voice came again, and still, they couldn't understand. The voice sounded a third time. This time "they did hear the voice, and did open their ears to hear it; and *their eyes were toward the sound thereof; and they did look steadfastly towards heaven, from whence the sound came*" (3 Nephi 11:5; emphasis added).

Only when they changed their focus could they hear the glorious voice of their Father in Heaven announcing the coming of His Son, their Savior, Jesus Christ. It was only when they looked up that they saw the Redeemer descending out of heaven.

Heavenly Father expects us to have good and righteous goals and plans and to always be anxiously engaged in a good cause (see D&C 58:27), but we cannot be so focused on what seems to be right in front of us that we cannot see the times when His will might be different.

I believe Heavenly Father has a plan for *all* of us and for *each* of us. Prayer, scripture study, and a purposeful choice to change our focus to that which is of an eternal nature help dim the light of our own will and illuminate His.

Even now God is orchestrating people and opportunities as well as experiences and blessings for us to enjoy here on earth. We must be careful that our own hopes, dreams, and desires are not so bright that we cannot see what lies beyond our mortal vision because there is more, so much more than what we can see in our own little rooms.

Relinquish Your Desires for His

When my kids were young, I would make great effort to avoid the toy aisles on our trips to the store. Invariably, the moment they caught wind of a toy, they wanted it. And to make matters worse, every time they turned their heads, they discovered something new they loved, needed, and *could not* survive without. It was interesting to see how quickly and easily each desired toy was replaced by the next as their eyes wandered down the aisle. Most of the time, they didn't even know what the toys did, but it didn't matter. They knew what they wanted, and the disappointment of not getting what they deemed was rightly theirs was, at times, too great to bear.

It's not uncommon to see kids crying, even screaming, at the store because they have been denied something they've desired. More than once, I was the mother strolling down the aisle with a screaming kid in tow. It wasn't fun. When my kids would try that, I wouldn't give in. "Screaming doesn't work," I would say. If they continued their fit, I would say, "Oh my, your fit tells me you didn't get enough sleep last night. You'll get to take a nap when we get home and go to bed early tonight." Then I would ignore whatever happened after that.

Not easy to do with a store full of raised eyebrows and judging frowns. They may have thought my kids were terrible and I was an awful mother. I should have just given them a lollipop to shut them up. Too bad. My kids weren't going to learn that fits got them what they wanted, especially when most of what they wanted was what they didn't need and would forget about after five minutes.

My kids eventually learned screaming didn't work and I wasn't going to give them what they wanted because they threw a fit. When they calmed down and shifted their focus to me, I was able not only to teach them *how* to get what they wanted (manners and kind words) but to try to teach them the tough principle that they didn't always get what they wanted because they didn't always want what was best for them. It was a tough lesson for them to learn as children—and still isn't easy as adults.

In my life, I've done my share of pouting when I haven't gotten my way, and maybe even thrown a fit or two, especially when I've thought what I've wanted is good and right. But I came to realize that right doesn't always mean right for me. Heavenly Father knows what is best for me, and He is waiting for me to quiet down so He can tell me.

The truth is it's human nature to want stuff, and getting what we want makes us happy. Whether it's a new purse, a new career, or a new toy, we find pleasure in the acquisition of our desires. We also have a natural tendency to hang on to stuff we don't need and maybe even some we don't even want. This is true across the board, from material goods to dreams to desires and to sins. We know what we want, and sometimes we simply don't want to let them go—until we make the decision to want something else.

One day, my husband made us nachos for a snack. He set the cheese-covered tortilla chips on the shared desk between us, and we snacked as we worked on our various computer tasks. I grabbed an extra-cheesy chip and said, "I love the cheesy ones," as I popped it into my mouth. Without reply or fanfare, my husband started taking chips from the bottom of the pile—the ones that had no cheese on them. I watched for a few minutes as he scooted aside the cheesy chips and grabbed the bare ones. I smiled and told him I saw what he was doing. He simply said, "It's because I love you."

Cheesy chips aren't vital to his existence, but they are one of his favorite things to eat. And he sacrificed them for me. The act itself was small, but the meaning behind it was enormous. He gave up something he loved because he loved me more, and I love him even more because of it.

I was watching a clip taken from a television show awhile back. It was a snippet of a conversation between a mother who was newly widowed and her adult daughter. The daughter had just discovered a fifteen-year-long affair her father had had. In spite of the knowledge of the affair from the beginning, her mother had stayed with him because she had loved him. The daughter, in an effort to comfort her grieving mother, said, "He did love you though."

The mother, brokenhearted, flatly replied, "But he didn't give up anything to do it. What kind of love is that?"

How profound. How sad. How true. He wasn't willing to give up his selfish desires for the sake of love.

This caused me to ask myself, how much do I love my Father in Heaven? How much do I trust Him? What am I willing to give up to show my love for Him, my commitment to Him? Am I willing to give up selfish desires and worldly appetites? Am I willing to give up pride? Am I willing to give up my will for His?

Yes, we love our Heavenly Father, but what are we giving up to follow Him and His will? Are we willing to give up our desire to micromanage every detail of the world around us? Are we willing give up blaming our own shortcomings on others? Are we willing to claim personal control and give the rest to Him because we trust Him and love Him?

I think of a story of a great king. Thousands looked to him, worshipped him. He had riches, servants, fame, and power. And yet there came a point in his life where he desired something more: to know God. On his knees, bowing before God, he pleaded, "I will give away all my sins to know thee" (Alma 22:18). A relationship with Heavenly Father became more important than any desire, habit, or sin. The king was willing to give up all he had, including his will, to know God.

The truth of the matter is this: God is the perfect choreographer, coordinator, artist, and father. He has perfect love for us. He has a perfect plan for us. Much like a college advisor knows what classes we must take to earn a degree, God knows what experiences we need to have to fulfill our potential. Some of these experiences might be difficult, but it's because "we must through much tribulation enter into the kingdom of God" (Acts 14:22).

It is through the refiner's fire that we are molded to be like Him. Pain is a necessary part of this life, but if we turn to Him and follow His will, He can help us avoid unneeded pain and consecrate our needed afflictions for our gain (see 2 Nephi 2:2).

While we must experience hard times, our very purpose is to have joy (see 2 Nephi 2:25). I believe Heavenly Father wants to lead us to those choices, people, opportunities, and experiences He knows will bring us that joy—things we might not be able to see without His help and guidance. As we seek out His will for us, our lives will take on greater meaning, richer context, and deeper joy than we could imagine.

Our Savior provided the perfect example of living His Father's will. Many times He told others, "I seek not mine own will, but the will of the Father which hath sent me" (John 5:30). He could have taken the credit for miraculous healings and heavenly teachings, but He never did. He could have shied away from the unimaginable pain and suffering of the Atonement, but He did not. In the Garden of Gethsemane, Jesus fell on His face and prayed, "O my Father, if it be possible, let this cup pass from me." If there was any other way . . . and yet He continued, "Nevertheless not as I will, but as thou wilt" (Matthew 26:39).

Having faith in Heavenly Father and listening for the promptings of the Holy Ghost aren't going to cut it if we are not willing to trust that His plan is better than ours. That would be like having faith in and listening to a tour guide but refusing to follow him because you don't want to leave the hotel lobby. Think of all you would miss!

If we trust Heavenly Father and relinquish our will to Him, we allow Him to open doors we cannot on our own. He is all-knowing *and* all-loving. He is also a respecter of agency and will not force Himself into our lives. Though there are times when He intervenes, He will never rob us of our agency. He will never take our will. It is ours to give. Of this Elder Neal A. Maxwell said, "The submission of one's will is really the only uniquely personal thing we have to place on God's altar. The many other things we 'give' . . . are actually the things He has already given or loaned to us. However, when you and I finally submit ourselves, by letting our individual wills be swallowed up in God's will, then we are really giving something to Him! It is the only possession which is truly ours to give!" (Maxwell, "Swallowed Up in the Will of the Father").

What a blessing that we have something we can give back to God! And here is where the great miracle lies: the more we give our will to His, the more our will becomes His. At first, we may want what is contrary to His teachings or His plan, but as we willingly give those up because we come to understand, love, and trust Him, we become more like Him. We find that our desires and goals

change as we grow, and more and more, what we choose for ourselves becomes what He would choose for us as well. Eventually,
living His will won't be a sacrifice to us because it will be our will
too. So when we think we are relinquishing something, in reality,
we are gaining everything.

Remember

The older I get, the more I'm convinced my mind isn't a steel trap;
it's a plastic colander, and each year the holes seem to get bigger. It's
becoming more and more difficult for me to recall the details of my
childhood, even teenage years. Sure, I remember the big stuff, but
much of it is simply gone. And I haven't just lost memories. I've lost
stuff. I don't know how many items I've put somewhere safe, where
I would never forget, only to forget where that somewhere safe was.
Even more sad, I've also lost lessons, impressions, and epiphanies.

That's why I write so much. I write in my scriptures. I've got
notebooks filled to the brim, and I've kept a journal since I was thir-
teen. I don't want to forget those thoughts and memories and impressions. The funny thing is on occasion I'll come across something
I've written and not remember writing it in the first place! But most
times, when I read what I have written, I remember. Pictures come
back to my mind, feelings come back to my heart, and a piece of my
past comes back to life. When I read my thoughts of a spiritual nature, like the notes in the margins of my scriptures, impressions and
insights I once gained reenter my soul, and I am filled again. Oh, the
power of remembering!

It's safe to assume Heavenly Father knows we won't remember
everything all the time, even really important things. He's very aware
of my colander brain. That's probably why the word *remember*, in
some form or fashion, shows up in the scriptures 497 times—so we
can be reminded of what is important.

You might wonder why I have chosen to add *remember* to the
list of how to give our will to God. The answer is simple: giving our
will to God is not just a one-time thing. It is a continual process, an
ongoing contribution. Sometimes we can forget to give our will to

Him, and we start to follow our own will. It's vital that we strengthen our ability to look back so we can remember our choice to live His will and get back on track.

In the Book of Mormon, there was a time of great spiritual awakening and growth. Great affliction reminded the people of their need for the Savior, and thousands were brought down into the waters of baptism. The Church grew, and the state of the people improved. With their riches came pride, and with pride came misplaced credit and desires. Alma, their spiritual leader, went out to teach them, to "preach the word of God unto them, to stir them up in remembrance" (Alma 4:19).

Alma didn't go about trying to teach them something new; his goal was to *remind* them of what they once knew. He asked them to *remember* the Lord's mercy and long-suffering and *remember* their redemption from hell through Him (see Alma 5:6). That call to remembrance "changed their hearts," and the Lord "awakened them out of a deep sleep, and they awoke unto God. Behold, they were in the midst of darkness; nevertheless, their souls were illuminated by the light of the everlasting word" (Alma 5:7). What beautiful imagery that creates that when we remember, we awake unto God.

Years ago, I decided to attend a women's conference at Brigham Young University. It was a two-day offering of dozens of classes and speakers on a variety of topics. I went with a very specific goal in mind: to strengthen my testimony of Jesus Christ as my Savior. I found myself uplifted and edified, but on the second day, I still hadn't received what I had come for. Elder Jeffrey R. Holland and his wife, Patricia, were the last speakers. Their words were good and wise, and I took copious notes. Then Elder Holland spoke alone, and something happened to me. My pen went still, but later that night I picked it up again and recorded the event:

Elder Holland addressed us. As an Apostle, from the pulpit, he bestowed upon each one of us attending an apostolic blessing. It was during this that I received an answer to my desire. I was overwhelmed by the Spirit. I have heard people say they were consumed by the Spirit. I have to say that I could easily use those words to describe how it felt.

It filled me from head to toe, like hot chocolate on a cold day. It filled me with the knowledge that Jesus Christ is my Savior. I knew it, and for the first time in my life, I would not have been more sure if He was standing right there before me.

I felt peaceful yet empowered; humble yet strong. I am so grateful for that experience. I hope I will be able to feel the Spirit testify to me of my Savior that strongly and succinctly again in my life, but I don't think I'll need it. Like everyone, I have good days spiritually and not-so-good days. In my not-so-good days, all I need to do is think about that experience, and I am again sustained.

That was an experience I knew I'd never forget. And since then, there have been some spiritually not-so-good days in which I've wondered if God sees me and if the Atonement really applies to me. And on those days, I go back and read this from my journal. Every time I have done that, those feelings I felt are born again, and I am refreshed.

Because I had this experience and I *remembered* it, there is no need for me to have it again. The Spirit testifies to me each time I *remember* that spring day in 2005 that, yes, He is very real, and He is my Savior. That's the power of remembering!

Remembering keeps our minds focused and our eyes pointed toward Him. As we try to allow Heavenly Father's will into our lives, we will experience wonderful growth, which He has orchestrated for us. We will meet people, give service, receive impressions, and find a greater level of purpose, peace, and joy. We might be tempted to call on Him less when life isn't going well or perhaps even develop pride in our blessed state. In times of discouragement and difficulty, we may fail to see His care and concern and pull ourselves away from Him as we wrap ourselves up in anger and sorrow. This is when the power of remembrance comes into the picture.

Remembering is illuminating. In the good and bad times, when we might not be feeling particularly close to Him, when we might forget His purpose and plan, when we just aren't seeing or feeling Him in our lives, we can remind ourselves that He is. We can think back to the times we knew He was with us and trust that He still is. We can reach back to the truths we once believed and trust that they are still true. We can look back and remember our decision to have faith, the impressions we've received, and the times we've refocused on Him and relinquished our desires for Him. We can remember why we made those choices and how we felt, and we can believe and feel that way again.

Our souls can once again be illuminated by His light, if we but just remember.

He's Got This

Have you heard the story about the young girl who took her mother's favorite brooch, wrapped it up, and gave it to her mother for her birthday? The mother smiled sweetly at her daughter and said, "What a sweet gesture, but . . . isn't this my brooch?"

The little girl beamed and replied, "It's yours, but I didn't have anything else to give you. Besides, it's the thought that counts, right?"

Though we can't *give* God control because it's already His, we can give Him our trust and our life. It's the thought that counts, right? Right. We essentially turn our lives over to Him like clay to a potter, trusting He will create something wonderful. We put our trust in Him that no matter what happens, He is over all.

That is not always an easy thing to do in light of what's going on in the world. Crime is common; the values of the world are shifting away from God's; natural disasters, illnesses, and accidents take lives; people use their agency for selfish and harmful activities. The world around us can be unpredictable and, at times, even scary. And though we don't know exactly what may come, through His prophets, Heavenly Father has given us an idea of the whole of it.

We are living in the winding-up times before the Second Coming of Jesus Christ. Our time has been prophesied of by the likes of John (see Revelation 14), Isaiah (see Isaiah 1, 2, 51, 52), Moroni (see Mormon 8), and more. We have a good idea of what is to come—calamity, temptation, distraction, etc. But we also know the exciting and wonderful events in store! We have an idea of the big picture, and through the inspiration of the Holy Ghost, Heavenly Father can offer us a personal tour through this life.

As we make the effort to seek His will and follow it, He can help us avoid pitfalls and dangers and give us strength when life calls for heavy lifting. He can help us see and hear things otherwise missed and share His mysteries with us. We can obtain peace, knowing He is there even though we cannot see Him. And as we learn to align our will with His and are willing to give up what doesn't match up, even if we think it's good—because His will is always better—we will find the fear and pride and the desires of the natural man will be cleared from our paths, and we will be able to follow Him where He wants us to go. And where He wants us to go might be tough but wonderful just the same.

When we think of giving up our will for Heavenly Father's, we tend to focus on the hardships in our lives. We focus on how we can find strength in our trials and purpose in our pain. But following God's will doesn't just help assuage suffering; it can also put us in good positions doing things we have never imagined possible. A willing tool will be put to work in the Master's hand!

We might find as we follow Him that we will become leaders or teachers or mothers or writers. We might be placed in situations that are so good we might not think we deserve to be there. We might wonder why bad things are happening to others, but not to us. We might doubt our ability and wonder what He was thinking.

When God sees fit to bless us with peace or prosperity, there is no need to ask why or feel undeserving. He doesn't make mistakes. I believe He is eager to give us as many positive experiences as possible. And living His will opens us to those wonderful blessings He has prepared for us. Some of those wonderful experiences might only be born out of our trials. We don't know, but He does. He knows all. He's got a plan. He's got this. And He is just waiting for us to believe it.

Chapter 6

The Perfect Companionship

*"I promise you that you will one day stand aside and
look at your difficult times, and you will realize
that He was always there beside you."*

—President Thomas S. Monson

The Perfect Companionship

When my kids were little, they did what I told them to out of a sense of obedience, and that made me happy. But the happiness was nothing compared to when they grew to be teenagers and came to me on their own and, after doing their best to figure out what was right, asked me what I thought they should do.

That brought me joy, not because I liked to be obeyed but because their actions were a reflection of their feelings for and about me. They still come to me for guidance because they love me and trust me. They also know I love them and would only counsel them to do what would be best for them. I feel closer to them and they to me. It makes me happy. It pleases me.

I can more than assume that as we go to the Lord for what He would have us do, it pleases Him as well. In His own words to those who seek His will, He says, "Behold, this is pleasing unto your Lord, and the angels rejoice over you" (D&C 88:2). Imagine that! When we seek God's will, it pleases Him and makes the angels rejoice. And why does it please Him so? Why does it make the angels rejoice? Because it is a sign of our love for Him, evidence of our trust and faith in His plan for us.

We know He has the power to guide and protect us, and our coming to Him allows Him to do that. He says, "For the Lord will go before you, and the God of Israel shall be your rearward" (3 Nephi 20:42). If we let Him, He will have our front and our back. If we do our part and follow His lead, beautiful things can happen.

Think of an orchestra, a ballet, or a choir. They are made of a collection of people dedicated to honing their skills. But rather than each person going their own way, they look to one conductor, choreographer, or director to bring them together. When the people and the plan come together in unison, it becomes a moving, beautiful, and exciting performance.

After we claim righteous responsibility for what lies in our personal control, give the rest of the control to God, and humbly accept His will in our lives, we come together with Him in unison, and our lives become moving, beautiful, and exciting stories. We create what I call the perfect companionship. We no longer are sole participants in our own play but are part of a team. We see, feel, and grow in a way we could not on our own.

The word *perfect* in perfect companionship doesn't mean we will be perfect. We aren't—and that's expected. *Perfect* applies to the position. When we do our part and allow God to do His, we put ourselves in the perfect position and place for heavenly aid and influence. Our lives will change, we will change, and our relationship with Him will change too.

As part of a team, we grow closer to God. Sister Anne C. Pingree experienced this as she reached for a perfect companionship with her Heavenly Father. She said, "In even the smallest details of each day, I submitted my will to the Lord's, for I so needed His help, His guidance, and His protection. As I did, gradually my relationship with my Father in Heaven changed—in profound ways" (Pingree, "Knowing the Lord's Will").

Perhaps this is what causes the angels to rejoice. Perhaps they rejoice because they know that when we enter into a perfect companionship with God, we open ourselves to a higher level of peace, understanding, strength, and joy. We are okay not having all the answers because we know He does. We can find solace when others lose their way because we know He loves them and is watching over them. We can see a purpose in our pain and afflictions as opportunities to work with Him, not be angry at Him. We choose to live our lives His way, with Him by our side. We can have peace and security in a crazy world. Yes, those are reasons to rejoice.

I love the story of the sweet farm boy named Westley who loves a young woman named Buttercup. She toys with him, delighting in the smallest of demands. Each time he answers with, "As you wish." It doesn't take her long to realize what he is really saying is, "I love you." She realizes then that she loves him too. It's a beautiful story, even the part where (spoiler alert) he dies. But don't worry; it's not permanent. They fight princes, rodents of unusual size, each other, and more before they reach their happily ever after.

As you wish. He did all she asked because he loved her. Her happiness was more important than his own. He was willing to forsake all to be with her. On a spiritual plane, I liken "As you wish" to "Thy will be done." When the Father's will is made known in a perfect companionship, we accept it because we love Him. His plan is more important than ours. We are willing to forsake all to be with Him again.

Heavenly Father wants to be our companion in our righteous endeavors of this life. In fact, that is one of the reasons He asks so much of us. I share once again the wisdom of President Lorenzo Snow: "The sacrifices that are required of us are of that nature that no man or woman could make them, unless aided by a supernatural power; and the Lord, in proposing these conditions, *never intended* that his people should ever be required to comply with them *unless by supernatural aid* . . . He has promised this aid" (*Teachings of Presidents of the Church: Lorenzo Snow*; emphasis added). We mustn't feel bad that we can't do it all on our own, because we are not meant to. It is His desire and plan that our lives not be solo endeavors but team endeavors—companionships.

Without question, the greatest and most perfect example is Jesus Christ. He exercised total and complete control over His priorities, His actions, His attitude, and His belief. From before the world was, when He answered the Father's call with the words, "Here am I, send me" (Abraham 3:27) to His entire mortal ministry to His seat in the heavens above next to His Father (D&C 137:3), Jesus Christ *lived* His Father's will.

When we talk about the sacrifice the Savior made for us, we often speak of how He gave up His life for us when He died for us, but there is another meaning as well. When Jesus Christ accepted His role as the Redeemer of mankind, He gave up the chance to have a "normal" life. Every decision He made in His lifetime pointed toward fulfilling His Father's will, not His own. He learned His role and responsibility by degrees from his infancy (see Luke 2:52). He gave up the chance to be completely mortal, to raise a family, to live to old age . . . to have someone else bear the burden of His sins. He gave up the chance to live a mortal existence like everyone else so He could live the life His Father would have Him live. He truly sacrificed all and gave all to be in a perfect companionship with our Father.

The scriptures are filled with many who tried to live in a perfect companionship with Heavenly Father. They endured hardship and loss, saw and performed miracles, could see in the darkest of hours, and had strength and joy that come only through an eternal perspective.

We read of people like Paul, who knew nothing in this life could separate him from the love of his God (see Romans 8:37–39), Peter, who taught the Apostles to obey God rather than men (see Acts 5:29), and Mary, who submitted to God with the sweet words,

"Behold the handmaid of the Lord; be it unto me according to thy word" (Luke 1:38). They responded to Him with their own "As you wish." Even though they were imperfect themselves, through their perfect companionship with Him, they did more and became more than they could have ever done on their own.

Each of them had to make the decision to live the life God had in store for them, lives that would be very different from the ones they had planned. Paul, once called Saul and who was a fervent persecutor of Christians, became one of the greatest missionaries of the New Testament. The fisherman Peter became the leader of Jesus Christ's Church on earth after Christ's Crucifixion and Resurrection. Mary, a young Jewish maiden, became the mother of the Savior of the world. They traded their plans for His, their lives for His life for them, and, in doing so, became partners in His great work and, in the end, their own salvation.

I was talking to Carol, a good friend, about the perfect companionship because she is someone I feel has one. She said, "I choose to be happy every day in my life, no matter what He sees fit for me, because I trust Him. I control what is in my power, then I take the rest, put it in a box, and lay it at His feet." It was a beautiful statement, but I'll admit, it conjured up a funny picture in my mind of me biting my lip as I laid a giant box, bow and all, on the floor and gently slid it apologetically toward Jesus. "Um, I think this is yours."

At first glance, it might not seem a very thoughtful gift— "Here you go. I have a hard enough time just keeping track of myself, so you worry about everything else."—but that is not the way it is. The gift isn't all of our worries and problems we don't want to deal with; the gift is our love, trust, and will. It is the way we tell Him we know there is a reason for *everything* and a purpose in all and we will do all we can to see it, do our part, and be grateful for it. Just the thought of it brings me a sense of relief and security. I am not alone, nor do I have to do this alone. He is with me, and I am with Him. And *together* I can live the life He and I want for me.

The butterfly is a popular symbol for metamorphosis, or change. Living in a perfect companionship can change us for the better. We start out as a ground-dwelling being, and through our own spiritual metamorphosis, we learn to fly. Having God as a companion changes us and makes us free.

Anyone can have a perfect companionship with God. The opportunity is not just for the people in the scriptures but for us today if we so desire. In fact, I'd like to introduce you to three women, friends of mine who exemplify the perfect companionship. They are imperfect and real. Their trials are heartbreaking and their faith inspiring. If anyone has reason to question God and His will, they do. But they don't. Rather, they choose to have a perfect companionship with Him.

Lavinda

I met Lavinda the spring of 1993 in a small town in Minnesota. Back then I was known as Sister Steed, a full-time missionary for The Church of Jesus Christ of Latter-day Saints. Lavinda was married and was a mother of three young children. She had a childlike faith and a wonderful laugh; I immediately loved her.

I kept in contact with her and discovered that her life was pretty typical. She had her ups and downs, her struggles here and there, but on the whole, she was going along at a pretty predictable pace—until 2001, when her husband, Joe, began to have trouble with his vision. The problem took them from an eye doctor to a university hospital as they tried to figure out what was causing his blurred vision. Then came the verdict: multiple sclerosis (MS). A newbie nurse's comment on their way out the hospital doors solidified their devastation. "Don't worry. You've still got about ten good years left."

Their lives were changed forever. It blew the wind out of her sails. Little did Lavinda know it was only the beginning.

Over the next seven years, Lavinda watched and supported her husband as he endured incomprehensible pain, most of which was unrelated to the MS that was changing his body. Joe underwent extensive shoulder and back surgeries. Then came the necrotizing fasciitis, a rare flesh-eating disease. A year after the surgery that peeled away Joe's dead flesh, the vicious bacteria returned again. A second surgery occurred, then a third when the necrotizing fasciitis attacked again.

A wife can only sit in a hospital waiting room so many times not knowing if she will see her husband again before she comes to a sense of fear, sorrow, and feebleness that only God can bring her back from. But Lavinda knew God was in control, so she turned to Him with all she had. Her heart softened, her shoulders strengthened, and her perspective brightened. The string of painful surgeries and recoveries was punctuated by sweet experiences of miracles of love, illuminating experiences she would never have had if she hadn't gone through such dark times. But it wasn't over.

In 2008, Lavinda's teenage daughter's head began to ache after a roller coaster ride at an amusement park. It ached every day. Soon the headaches combined with migraines. They would come on quickly and intensely, often to the point of debilitation. Lavinda took her daughter to doctor after doctor, even to a specialist across the country, where Lisa was diagnosed with chronic daily headaches. They explained that the jarring of the roller coaster had caused whiplash. Though the initial injury had long since healed, the nerves in her brain were still firing pain signals. There was nothing they could do to make the pain go away. It would be a permanent condition.

Even though Lisa attended a pain management program, the headaches continued to worsen to the point that her body could no longer handle the pain. That was when the blackouts began. A blackout is a temporary but complete loss of vision that can occur sometimes for hours, sometimes days, and sometimes weeks.

It is one thing for a wife to see her husband suffer from known causes but a completely different experience to witness her child suffering, especially when no one knows why. A mother is supposed to take care of her children, fix them when they are hurting or afraid, make all the bad things go away. But Lavinda couldn't. That ache and her love for her daughter were the driving forces behind

Lavinda's search for answers from above. *What should I do? What doctor should we see now? Where should we go? What should I say? What can I do to make it better?*

What she didn't understand at the time was she had already given Lisa the one thing she needed—her faith. Lisa once shared, "I never questioned Heavenly Father's plan for me. I never asked why. I just had faith that I would be okay. I knew Heavenly Father was taking care of me. Within our trials, we must all find courage and faith to keep fighting. I can stand and say with confidence that I know trials are for our good if we have patience and bear them well. We must lean on our Father in Heaven to guide us in our lives. He will keep surprising us by showing us He wants to make us more than we've ever dreamed we could be."

In 2011, ten years after Joe's initial MS diagnosis and three years after Lisa's head began to ache, Lavinda offered a prayer of gratitude to Heavenly Father. She thanked Him for the strength and support He had given her and acknowledged once again His hand in all things. "Thank you," she whispered, "for giving me the health and strength I need to take care of everyone else." She knew she had a heavy load to bear, but she was grateful she had the strength to do it.

A morning not long after her prayer, Lavinda awoke with numbness in her arm, neck, and face. The doctors suspected and confirmed a disc herniation in her neck, and they scheduled a surgery. A final presurgery MRI, however, revealed an additional diagnosis. Lavinda had multiple sclerosis. Her immediate reaction was shock and anger. It seemed unfair; it felt like too much. How could she take care of everyone else if she was sick? What was God thinking now? What was she going to do now?

She shared with me the answers she soon found. "When I realized this was God's will and aligned my will with His, the question was am I going to follow or fight it?" She knew it was her choice, and she chose to follow it. She chose to live in perfect companionship with God. Through this companionship, Lavinda has developed a keen appreciation for the good times and the bad. "My challenges are meant for me to learn, to help me reach beyond what I think I can do."

This doesn't mean it's been an easy road for her family or for her. There have been times of mourning, sorrow, tears, and anger. During the almost unbearable times, she learned to keep going. "We take whatever we are given and simply manage it one day at a time."

Her choices allow her to see beauty and purpose in a life beyond her control. "The silver lining in all this," she said to me, "is that these experiences bring more knowledge, understanding, and wisdom than I could have known otherwise." Some of the sweetest talks she and her husband have shared have been while she has been pushing him in a wheelchair around the hospital grounds. And some of the most tender times she has had with her daughter have been when she has served as her eyes. In experiences like these, Lavinda says, "We have found joy."

Despite the odds, Lavinda's family is doing quite well. As of this writing, Joe is doing better than before his diagnosis. He developed a passion for cycling a few years ago, and though his health often dictates his rides, it doesn't dictate his attitude and determination. He has a deep and abiding love of life, God, and his sweet wife.

After years of continual pain and spending more time blind than seeing, Lisa is close to discovering the cause of her illness. In the meantime, however, she has met and married a wonderful young man and is inspiring many with her story and testimony.

And Lavinda? She is doing well too. There have been struggles, and she has battled with fear of the unknown. But she has embraced the words, "So what if?" So what if she ends up in a wheelchair? So what if she never improves? So what? If she is living God's will, He will take care of her. She has made the choice to truly let go of fear and embrace Him, diving into the scriptures and listening for inspiration—trusting Him. The things that once seemed huge now seem small, if you can imagine that.

The word *challenge* seems inadequate in describing her life, but through it all, she has kept the childlike faith and laughter I loved so much years ago. Her words of affirmation still linger in my ears: "Life is good. Life is great!" God is good, and so are they, is her testimony. Of which she says, "What would I do without my testimony, Michelle? It's what gives me strength to carry on. It's what makes sense of my life. I mean, it and my family are what make me happy." And happy she is indeed.

Carol

I was asked to speak at an adult-only Church meeting a while ago. As I sat on the stand, I glanced over to the other people who had been invited to speak—a lovely older woman, a man about my age, and a slender, beautiful young woman. The young woman kept her eyes fixed on her clasped hands in her lap. I figured she was mortified and was still trying to figure out why she was asked to speak and what she would possibly speak on.

I should have known better.

When she got up to speak, she clasped both sides of the pulpit as she adjusted her weight. That was when I noticed she didn't have feet. They were prosthetics. Then I realized she wasn't clasping both sides of the pulpit because she was missing a hand. I felt a wave of shame for my initial assessment of her. She had a story to tell, one that I, without even hearing her speak, wanted to know.

Her name was Carol Decker. In 2008, when she was eight months pregnant with her second child, she got sick with a cold. Her cold turned to pneumonia, which then became sepsis. Sepsis occurs when the chemicals released into the bloodstream to fight infection trigger an inflammatory response instead. Rather than fighting her illness, her body turned on itself. In Carol's case, it attacked her vital organs and her skin. She was rushed into an emergency C-section, after which she experienced yet another complication: disseminated intravascular coagulation. Basically, it meant her blood began clotting where it shouldn't and didn't where it should. Again, vital organs, muscles, skin, and tissues were all affected. The odds were stacked against her.

Her body fought hard, and she lived but not without casualties.

She lost both legs from the calves down, her left hand, and her ring finger from her right hand. She also lost her sight. Though she lived through the experience, she would never see her second daughter. She would never see her husband or first daughter again. She couldn't see the people she was speaking to, and she didn't see me crying behind her.

Since then, Carol has become a fast and dear friend and one of the greatest women I know. She has shared with me the story of her excruciating recovery, where she plummeted into the darkest places emotionally, spiritually, and physically. But somehow she came out the other side with a testimony, gratitude, and a smile. One day I asked her how she can have such a great attitude and love for life, considering her challenges. She said, "When I got out of the hospital and came home, I wanted to die. After a couple weeks of that, I realized something—that I wasn't going to die, that I didn't want to die. I made the decision then that I was going to fight, to live. And not just live but live a full life and be happy."

That decision ignited a fire in her that lit the way for her recovery physically, spiritually, and emotionally. Through years of pain, therapy, and hard work, Carol has lived her dream: being the best mom she ever could be. She cooks with her daughters, plays with them, sings to them, and loves them. They and her good husband are her world, and she says everything else is just a bonus. I am continually amazed by the attitude and gratitude she has chosen to have. Awhile back, she called me and excitedly told me about her new prosthetics. "For the first time, I feel like I have feet again. Yesterday I danced around the house with my girls! It was wonderful!"

Carol is a powerful example of having a perfect companionship. Her life was changed dramatically. It wasn't her choice or her plan. It just was. Yet she understood it was up to her what she did with her new life. She made a purposeful decision to be positive and have a good attitude, to *want* this new life. She chose to let go of anger and self-pity. She chose to trust that God could help her find a reason and a purpose—that He is ultimately in control. She claimed personal control, gave the rest to Him, and embraced her new life with passion, purpose, gratitude, and joy.

One day, I confessed to her my initial thoughts about her that night at the meeting. She laughed so hard she nearly dropped the phone. That wasn't a surprise; Carol laughs a lot. Her laughter inspires me and makes me love my life more. Not because my life is better or worse but because she has shown me that no matter what life brings, it can be loved. And that's where the joy is.

Bonnie

"I want to be angry at someone, anyone. The most logical finger-pointing I could do is at the Lord. But even then, I can't be mad or angry at Him. He has a plan. I trust Him in that He knows what's best for me and my family. Everything happens for a reason and according to His plan. The only thing we can control in these situations is how we react to them. I can't be mad."

Those are the words of my dear friend Bonnie. She is one of those people who comes into your life and fills a hole you didn't know was there, a person your heart tells you is not just a friend but a sister.

The first time I met Bonnie was on my way to a writer's retreat in Washington State. My friend and I picked her and a few others up at the airport. Petite and accommodating, Bonnie sat on the raised middle backseat bench between two other ladies. I was amazed to learn an hour into our two-hour drive that Bonnie was six months pregnant.

She was folded up so tightly in the backseat that I couldn't even see her baby bump. We tried to move her to another seat, but she wouldn't budge. "I'm okay, really." I was impressed with her easy-going ways and her attitude. When I was pregnant, I would swell up like a water balloon and would only be comfortable when I was spread eagle with a fork in my hand. Bonnie simply smiled at me from the backseat, and I knew then that I loved her. It didn't take me long to learn that her words, "I'm okay, really," were not just good manners but were lyrics for her life.

A few months after our retreat, Bonnie and I were excitedly planning to room together at a writer's conference in Arizona, her neck of the woods. But the birth of her second son—the baby bump in the backseat—changed that. It changed everything.

Bonnie's son was born with trisomy 13, a chromosomal disorder with a high mortality rate. This was a surprise to her and her husband, as well as the doctors and nurses. Aside from Bonnie's not gaining much weight the last few weeks of pregnancy, there had been no indication of abnormality or distress. But there he was—a full head of hair, a cleft lip and pallet, and calm, focused eyes that told his mother he knew exactly who she was.

After four days in the hospital, Bonnie, her husband, and their two-year-old son took their newest addition home. For how long, they didn't know. They spent the next hours and days together feeding, playing, nurturing, and loving. When his time approached, his parents rocked him in their arms and sang hymns and lullabies. His breath came and went for the last time on his eighth day of life; he passed through the veil and went home.

Rather than seeing Bonnie at the writer's conference that weekend, I saw her at her son's viewing. When I approached her, she smiled, hugged me, and asked how I was doing. Oh, sweet Bonnie. I asked her how she was. She answered through a teary smile, "I'm okay, really." I knew she wasn't. How can you be with your child lying next to you in a casket? It just didn't make sense. I searched for the truth behind her red eyes, and I saw a glimmer of peace. I knew if she wasn't okay then, she would be.

We've had many conversations since then. She's shared feelings of sorrow, mourning, fear, and loss. But she has also shared with me her faith in God and His plan. Though she still longs to know why her son had to go home, she trusts that Heavenly Father has His reasons. And someday He will tell her. "I have to fully trust that He has a plan for each and every one of us," she once said. "Whether or not we understand it or want to find the reason for things, we need to trust that He knows what's best. It's not an easy thing, especially when life doesn't go the way we think or would like it to go. So the big question is am I willing to let go of the control and trust that the Lord loves me, is guiding me, and knows what's best for me?"

Three months after the viewing, she and I attended a writer's conference in Utah together. It was the first time she had been away from her husband and oldest son. Though she was in another state, her mind and heart were at home. On the first day, we drove around and talked awhile before grabbing some dinner. She told me something surprising. She wasn't mad. She had tried to be, but she just couldn't be mad at God. In fact, some people were mad at her for not being mad, but she couldn't do it. Deep in her core, she knew God had a plan, loved her dearly, and was taking care of her son.

Bonnie had every reason to call foul, demand answers, and scream injustice. She could have allowed anger and bitterness to fester. But she didn't. Bonnie is another moving example of a woman in a perfect companionship with her Father in Heaven. She understands with painful clarity that she isn't in control of what happens, but she does know that she can control how she responds. And she knows, loves, and trusts the One that is in control.

In her words, "Having a child return home earlier than we would like is not an easy thing. It makes one think, learn, trust, question, and so much more. Many may want answers as to why or what will come. I was blessed to not necessarily have those exact questions but to trust the Lord knows what He's doing. As for the why, we are all entitled to our own personal revelation in any situation. However, we most likely will not receive the answer when we want it. It is always on His time table, not ours. As hard as that is, it does make things easier. Someday, when the time is right, I will understand the why behind things. But for now, I trust the Lord."

She still does.

You Don't Have to Be Perfect

Lavinda, Carol, and Bonnie are powerful examples of a perfect companionship. They are in the process of claiming personal control as they decide how they respond and what they believe and actively choose joy and God in their lives. They have also come to understand what it means to let go and give the rest to God. They trust that He has a purpose and a plan. They know that when He feels they are ready, they will have all the answers. And even though they don't know all things, they, like Nephi, know that God loves them (see 1 Nephi 11:17), and that is good enough for now.

There is something really important I'd like to make clear: you don't have to go through something as dramatic or traumatic in your life as these women have to have a perfect companionship with God. I share the stories of Lavinda, Carol, and Bonnie because the weight of their trials makes it easier to see the relief that comes from claiming personal control and giving Him the rest.

Though I've been through some tough times in my life, I've never had to deal with anything on the level these strong women have. Sometimes it's hard not to compare myself to them and feel like a loser when I complain about my life. I mean, here are these amazing women who have overcome such tremendous loss and hardship, and I get upset because I'm overweight and uncoordinated. Suddenly my issues seem so small, and so do I. In fact, I was talking with Carol about this very thing when she said, "Don't think that, Michelle. I am just like you, and you would do just what I did if you were in my shoes—no pun intended." How I love that woman!

In fact, none of these women feels she has done anything significant or sees anyone else's life as easier. Bonnie put it so well when she said, "Life never brings what we expect. Nobody's experiences are ever exactly the same. And who are we to say that we've had it harder than others? There are always people who have had something harder or something easier than we have."

All of us have a story to tell. We have all struggled, questioned, and cried, whether it's been over illness, family problems, divorce, health, financial troubles, addiction, wayward family members, natural disasters, accidents—the list can go on and on. Life is filled with hard trials to overcome. But here is the positive message I hope you take away: though we were born into an unpredictable and stormy world, we have been given the power to adjust our sails. And we have the opportunity to weather the storm *with* the One who knows all, who can strengthen our shoulders, lighten our load, clarify our perspective, and deepen our joy. Those are truths to rejoice in. That is a life to celebrate!

Yes, life can be hard. It's supposed to be. My good friend Trent recently said, "Life is a gym, not a day spa. So we shouldn't be surprised when we were expecting a massage but got handed weights." Life is a time for challenge and growth, and that isn't always easy.

When my kids complained about how hard something was, I would often say, "Hard isn't the same thing as bad." Yes, life is hard. That is a universal fact. But it is also good. In fact, it's *really* good. We have the opportunity to experience mortality! We can love and work and laugh and play and serve and build a family and eat brownies. We have the chance to be tested and tried and to overcome. And that is the expectation—we will overcome. The Lord Himself said, "He that is faithful and endureth shall overcome the world" (D&C 63:47).

But there's more than just overcoming our trials on earth. The Lord explained, "He that endureth in faith and doeth my will, the same shall overcome, and shall receive an inheritance" (D&C 63:20). And what is our inheritance? Everlasting life (see Matthew 19:29), a place prepared in the mansions of the Father (see Ether 12:34), the kingdom of heaven (see D&C 6:37), the kingdom of God (see 2 Nephi 9:18), the earth (see Matthew 5:5), and all things (see D&C 78:22). Heavenly Father wants and is willing to give us all that is His, but we must choose to accept that gift, to want it too, and to work for it. A gentleman in church once said, "We can have eternal life if we want it. But *only* if there is nothing we want more."

Is there anything we want more than eternal life? Than the inheritance God wants to give us? Of course we'd say no, but if we want to obtain eternal life, we have to want it more than we want to hold on to our pity, anger, fear, selfishness, and pride. If we want to have all that He has in store for us, we have to want to adhere to His will more than we want to try to control the world around us.

We want that because we choose to believe He can offer us more than anything the world can offer us.

Being in a perfect companionship doesn't mean we are perfect. His job is to be perfect. Ours is to invite Him to be our companion in this life, to trust Him, to seek Him, to follow Him, to thank Him, and to try to be like Him. We do our part, and He will take care of the rest.

A Closing Word about Will

I was having a conversation with my dad and he brought up a really good point. He said, "When we give up our will, we actually aren't giving up anything, because if we knew what He knows about us, our lives, and His eternal plan, chances are it would be our will too."

I liked that statement, and the more I thought about it, I grew to love it. I can't tell you how many times my kids have second-guessed something I have suggested or tried to rebel against something I've asked them to do only for me to come back with the good old, "Just trust me. I'm the parent. I've been there. I know what I'm talking about. You won't regret it." It makes total sense on my end what I'm asking them to do, but their limited knowledge base and life experience doesn't always allow them to see it. Hence the words "Trust me."

As mortal beings on earth, our knowledge base of eternal things is certainly limited, and so is our life experience. We are all pretty new at this stuff. On the other hand, Heavenly Father has perfect and unlimited knowledge. He knows everything that has happened, is happening, and will happen. He also has quite a bit more life experience than we have. He *knows* what He's talking about. Sometimes it's hard for us to listen. We second-guess or try to rebel. We tirelessly petition Him with our own agenda, trying to bend His will to ours as if we have come up with the perfect solution or scenario that somehow slipped past Him. We just want to be happy, that's all. And we think we know what will make us happy. Sometimes we might be right. But all of the time He is right.

He listens to our plans and petitions and waits for us to stop talking long enough for us to hear Him. Then He guides and influences us through the Holy Ghost and other tender mercies to what will bring us not only happiness but also joy. He does this because He can see what we can't. He can see everything, and we won't regret trusting Him.

One of my favorite things I hear my kids (and my husband) say—right after I love you—is, "You were right." I don't know why. It just tickles my soul! Like the time I was pregnant with our first child and my husband wanted to buy a teeny, tiny two-door car. Thinking ahead to the bulky car seat and baby supplies we'd have to haul in and out of the car, I said I thought the four-door would be a better choice. We got the two-door. It wasn't a year later that the magical day came when my husband tried to pull the car seat out of the back for the millionth time when he turned and said, "You were right. We should have gotten a four-door." Music to my ears!

Surprisingly, I have found something even sweeter than my young children or my husband acknowledging my rightness. It is the sound of my teenage son's deep voice when he says, "Yeah, I guess you're right." Cue angelic choir singing.

My father wrote a poem during a time of searching for answers in his life called "The Will of God."

> *The will of God for me*
> *Would be my will for me*
> *If I knew about myself*
> *What God knows.*
>
> *To follow His will*
> *is not to surrender, but to trust;*
> *is not to lose identity, but to perfect its potential;*
> *is not to sacrifice agency, but to use it at its best.*
> *To follow His will*
> *is to trade my incomplete knowledge for His complete knowledge;*
> *is to trade my imperfect love of self for His perfect love for me;*
> *is to trade my flawed course of action for His perfect course of action.*

To follow His will
is to be in tune with reality,
is to know peace now, joy later,
is to fill the measure of my creation,
is to walk in the light,
is to never be alone.

The will of God for me
Fills best the longings of my soul
And brings me home
Whole and clean;
More than the child that left,
Less than the God to be,
But worthy to be at one
With they who are love.

Chapter 7

PEACE—What We Really Want

"No woman is a more vibrant instrument in the hands of the Lord than a woman of God who is thrilled to be who she is."

—Sheri L. Dew

Peace

Here is a thought that might come as a surprise to you—it did to me when I first realized it: *we think we want control, but what we really want is peace.*

If I were teaching this in front of a class, I would repeat it for effect. *We think we want control, but what we really want is peace.* Then I would stand quietly at the front of the room while you let that thought roll around and settle into your mind. It's an interesting concept, and it's true.

My son, Spencer, was always pretty independent. That is, until he started elementary school. He did not like to be away from his family. Kindergarten brought pretty typical behavior, and we did what we could to help the situation. He had good days and not-so-good days. I had good days and not-so-good days. Some days we were able to say good-bye with smiles, and others I had to leave him crying with his teacher while I drove home crying. He loved school, but he had a hard time not being home. He wanted to be in both places but couldn't.

As a mom, I really struggled. I wanted so badly for Spencer not to be sad and not to struggle. I did everything I could to help him. I made picture books of us for him to take to school, put notes in his lunch box, and asked his teacher if he could call home on the days that were particularly difficult for him. Jerey and I thought it was something Spencer would simply outgrow, but he didn't.

Finally, one morning, I realized that despite my best efforts, I could not fix the situation. I couldn't make Spencer's sadness go away. I couldn't control the situation, and it killed me. I asked him if he wanted to be homeschooled. He said no. He wanted to be at school; he just didn't like to not be at home. Realizing there was nothing I could do was hard. There's not a worse feeling as a mother than the feeling of helplessness.

I supported him in his desire to attend school and eventually even got a job at the school to be near him. When I took that step, Spencer stopped struggling with the separation. He worked hard, gained confidence and friends, maintained a positive attitude, and overcame his difficulty.

Spencer figured out that he could carry my love and support with him wherever he went. Our love for each other is a reflection of God's love for us. No matter where we are, His love is there. In this sense, no matter the distance between us, we can always feel close and connected. No matter what our trials are, He is there to support us. We are never alone. It's a truth that brings joy and comfort but one that is often misunderstood.

Paul knew that many people would feel distanced from God. He offered these encouraging words: "I am persuaded, that neither death, nor life, nor angels, nor principalities, nor powers, nor things present, nor things to come, nor height, nor depth, nor any other creature, shall be able to separate us from the love of God, which is in Christ Jesus our Lord" (Romans 8:38–39).

What a statement! Nothing, beyond our own choices, can separate us from Heavenly Father, Jesus Christ, and their love. No matter what difficulties lie in our paths, no matter what others choose to do, no matter how hard life gets, nothing can separate us from God's love.

Hopefully Paul's promising words will help our faith improve over time. We can learn through experience the truthfulness of what he said: no matter what separates us physically, nothing can separate us from the love we have for each other. It can give us comfort when we are away and the courage to take care of our own responsibilities surrounded by our family's continual love and support.

We can also find peace in the perfect companionship. Consider the Serenity Prayer:

> "God grant me the serenity
> To accept the things I cannot change;
> Courage to change the things I can;
> And the wisdom to know the difference."

Serenity is tranquility, peace. Peace comes when we accept what we can't change (give it to God), have the courage to change what we can (personal control), and have the wisdom to know the difference (embracing the balance of control). We can have that peace of mind and heart in a perfect companionship with God because despite the unpredictable elements of an imperfect world, some things are certain:

We can be certain that anywhere we are in life, in any circumstance or situation, *we can be in control of ourselves.*

We can be certain that no matter where we end up or what we go through, *God is beside us, our loving and active companion.*

No matter what this life brings, if we choose God, we will not only be okay, but we will also be victorious.

Those are certain. Throughout our lives, the scenery will change, but the characters and those scenarios never will. It does not matter if we are accepting an award or are in a cancer ward, raising small children or adopting teenagers, losing a job or gaining an education, are popular or are outcasts; we can be certain that we have the power in all of these situations to decide what is important to us, how we respond, what kind of attitude we will have, and what we will choose to believe.

We can also be certain that God will consecrate our struggles for our good, guide us to the people and places He has prepared for us, strengthen us, and always, always love us. We can know that regardless of what the world throws at us, now and in the end, with God's help, we will triumph. The scenery of our lives is ever changing, but these fundamental elements of a perfect companionship never change. There is no greater certainty, and in that, we can have no greater peace of mind.

Peace is a good and righteous desire, and how blessed are we to know how and where we can find it. Paul taught, "God is not the author of confusion, but of peace" (1 Corinthians 14:33). When we look to God, we can find peace.

To the sinning woman who bathed Christ's feet with her tears, the Savior said, "Thy faith hath saved thee; go in peace" (Luke 7:50). He could have offered her a place in heaven, cleanliness, happiness, and more, but He sent her on her way with the deepest longing of her heart: peace.

Jesus spoke to His Apostles at the Last Supper, saying, "Peace I leave with you, my peace I give unto you: not as the world giveth, give I unto you. Let not your heart be troubled, neither let it be afraid" (John 14:27). The Savior knew His time with them was coming to an end. He had just given them the power of the Holy Ghost (see John 14:26) so they could hear the will of God and follow Him. He had also exhorted them to claim personal control: "Love one another" (John 13:34), "Believe in God, believe also in me" (John 14:1), "Keep my commandments" (John 14:15), "Be of good cheer" (John 16:33).

He solidified their perfect companionship when He said, "These things I have spoken unto you, that in me ye might have peace. In the world ye shall have tribulation: but be of good cheer; I have overcome the world" (John 16:33). Then, after His disciples watched Him be killed and buried in the tomb, the risen Jesus Christ greeted them with, "Peace be unto you," not once but twice (John 20:19, 21).

In speaking of seeking the path to peace, President Monson offered three steps:

Search inward

Reach outward

Look heavenward (Monson, "The Path to Peace").

Sound familiar? Search inward—personal control. Reach outward—give the rest to God. Look heavenward—have a perfect companionship with God. It's the path to peace in the balance of control, accountability, and faith.

Peace in a Balanced Life

As you embrace the balance of control, you will not only survive, but you will thrive as well. Yes, life can be scary. We can feel out of control, unsure, and unbalanced. The adversary wants us to believe that is all true. He wants us to be afraid, to doubt ourselves and God. He wants us to think and feel the worst. He wants us to lose.

But we won't. We can have peace in a balanced life. We live *on* purpose *with* purpose; we own ourselves and trust God. We replace fear with faith in ourselves and Him because we know we have total control of our joy, our character, our testimony, and our future, and we know He has the rest. We know what we can do and what He will do. We know who He is, and we know who we can be. And we know how we can find peace and control in a world that can feel just the opposite.

As we learn and understand what we have control over, we begin to see that we have the power to overcome any trial, adversity, opposition, or affliction that may come our way. No one can take those things from us. We *own* them. Not only that, but as we claim personal control, we also put ourselves in the position to gain wonderful opportunities, experiences, relationships, and circumstances He has prepared for us. This wisdom and understanding can bring great joy.

In our perfect companionship, we know that no matter where we find ourselves in this unpredictable life we can't control, He is there with us. He is in charge. He has a plan. I've heard it said that if God brought us to it, He will bring us through it. That is so true. He loves us. He trusts us. He believes in us.

Own yourself. Trust Him. Have peace in a beautifully balanced life.

Works Cited

Buddha. *Dhammapada*. Kandy, Sri Lanka, 1985. <http://www. buddhanet.net/pdf_file/scrndhamma.pdf>.

Frankl, Viktor. *Man's Search for Meaning*. New York: Pocket Books, 1976.

Grassli, Michaelene P. "I Will Follow God's Plan for Me." *Ensign*, November 1988.

Hinckley, Gordon B. "God Hath Not Given Us the Spirit of Fear." *Ensign*, October 1984.

—. "Stand Strong Against the Wiles of the World." *Ensign*, November 1995.

Holland, Jeffrey R. "Lord, I Believe." *Ensign*, May 2013.

—. "Sanctify Yourselves." *Ensign*, May 2000.

Kimball, Spencer W. *Faith Precedes the Miracle*. Salt Lake City: Deseret Book Company, 1976.

Lindbergh, Anne Morrow. *Gifts from the Sea*. New York: Random House, 1975.

Maxwell, Neal A. "The Tugs and Pulls of the World." *Ensign*, November 2000.

—. "Swallowed Up in the Will of the Father." *Ensign*, November 1994.

Mclean, Michael. "What Part is Mine?" Sung by Felicia Sorensen.

Monson, Thomas S. "Living the Abundant Life." *Liahona*, January 2012.

—. "Your Personal Influence." *Ensign*, May 2004.

—. "The Path to Peace." *Ensign*, May 1994.

—. "Be of Good Cheer." *Ensign*, May 2009.

Packer, Boyd K. "Agency and Control." *Ensign*, May 1983.

—. "What Is Faith?" in *Faith* (1983), 42. Quoted and cited by Larry W. Gibbons, "A Time for Faith, not Fear." *Ensign*, July 2013.

—. "The Light of Christ." *Ensign*, April 2005.

Pearce, Virginia H. "Fear." *Ensign*, November 1992.

Pingree, Anne C. "Knowing the Lord's Will for You." *Ensign*, November 2005.

Richards, LeGrand. "A Testimony through the Holy Ghost." *Improvement Era*, June 1966.

Rose, Anne Marie. "Facing Trials with Optimism." *Ensign*, May 1996.

Rotter, Julian B. *Social Learning and Clinical Psychology*. New Jersey: Prentice-Hall, 1954.

Smart, Elizabeth, and Chris Stewart. *My Story*. New York: St. Martin's Press, 2013.

Teachings of Presidents of the Church: Joseph Smith. Salt Lake City: The Church of Jesus Christ of Latter-day Saints, 2012.

Teachings of Presidents of the Church: Lorenzo Snow. Salt Lake City: The Church of Jesus Christ of Latter-day Saints, 2012.

ten Boom, Corrie. *The Hiding Place*. Old Tappan, New Jersey: Fleming H. Revell Company, 1971.

The Princess Bride. Directed by Rob Reiner. 1987.

Wirthlin, Joseph B. "Come What May and Love It." *Ensign,* November 2008.

About the Author

MICHELLE WILSON LOVES GOD, HER family, laughter, and chocolate—pretty much in that order. She also loves to share gospel principles with a large dose of reality and a side of humor. She believes every woman has a unique purpose, divine worth, and awesome and very real possibilities. She enjoys speaking to groups large and small, writing, baking, spending time with family, seeing others succeed, and smiling. Michelle lives in Washington State with her husband, Jerey, their three children, two dogs, one cat, a hamster, a bunny, and homemade-ice-cream maker.